"Inside everyone there is a long

We are made in the image of

mobile, individualistic, cluttered world ... community is an endangered thing. And community is like working out—it takes work, sweat, discipline ... without that our muscles atrophy. Everybody wants to be fit, but not too many people want to do the work to get there. Mark's book is sort of a workout manual, helping you rediscover your communal muscles and start building them up slowly. It is an invitation to live deep in a shallow world." - **Shane Claiborne**, author and activist.

"Mark Votava's book is like a smooth stone in a churning stream. When all around us seems prone to speed, consumption, movement and success, *The Communal Imagination* is a sure and unwavering call to simplicity, presence, attentiveness and collaboration.. Read it slowly. It calls us to nothing less than a new way of being human." - **Michael Frost**, author of *Incarnate* and *The Road to Missional.*

"Embracing community is not simply a strong Christian value in which we all just try to get along, but rather is about becoming, together, the presence of Christ to one another and the world. Mark Votava invites us into that possibility in this book, in parts equally practical, personal and prophetic. It is high time for us to rediscover *The Communal Imagination.*" - **Jamie Arpin-Ricci**, author of *The Cost of Community*

"Some writers are widely read but live thinly; others read little but live deeply. In page after page of *The Communal Imagination*, my friend Mark Votava evidences the rare gift of being one who reads widely and lives deeply. Mark's careful but tenacious wisdom—forged in adventures of the glorious mundane of neighborhood gospel life—kindles me with hope and gratitude. May these pages likewise gift your community with eyes to see together what God may be up to." - **Brandon Rhodes**, D.Min., author of *Blip: Faithful Presence Amid the Making and Unmaking of the Petrol-Driven Church* (Spring 2015), Field Guide for the Parish Collective, owner of Rolling Oasis Grocers.

"Words like simplicity, vulnerability and humility are hard to find and harder to live in today's individualistic, high speed pursuit of success and control. Nonetheless, Mark Votava not only writes about them but intentionally and authentically embodies them in his everyday life in the parish. With warmth, honesty and a wonderful integration of Scripture reflections and true stories, Mark presents components of a communal imagination such as love, forgiveness and gratitude that challenge our current modes of being and invite us to embrace a way of life together that embodies the shalom of God's Kingdom. This book is not just for reading, it's for doing!" - **Karen Wilk**, Forge Canada National Team and Neighbourhood Mission Catalyzer, author of *Don't Invite Them To Church: Moving From a Coma and See to a Go And Be Church*.

"Many have written on the church as local presence, few have explored its depths with such first person intensity as Mark Votava. In *The Communal Imagination* Votava propelled me into his personal journey in a way that grew my capacity to be 'with' people I did not think possible. With wisdom and grace, the book challenged my life. It gave me a 'practice-based theology' for taking the gospel local." - **David Fitch**, BR Lindner Chair of Evangelical Theology, Northern Seminary, author of *Prodigal Christianity*.

"Rooted in intellect and experience, this book is a charge for the Church to reorient its identity from an autonomous entity to an interconnected organism. Acknowledging the high cost of such a reorientation, Mark offers a vision and set of practices that might just allow us to experience life and faith as it was meant to be lived." - **Jon Huckins**, neighborhood practitioner and author of *Thin Places*.

"Mark Votava wrestles with 'the tension between the real and the possible' in his Tacoma neighborhood, in community relationships and inside of himself. His humble witness invites us to consider and practice simplicity, love, growth, and gratitude. This profoundly honest text is chock full of ideas born of experience. A battle with depression, an intentional choice to leave employment as a school teacher and instead take jobs as a janitor and a dishwasher and the struggle to overcome anger and bitterness give him the authority to bring relevant recommendations. Votava's wise words on forgiveness, reconciliation and letting go of control have the ring of one who knows. This book covers essential territory for building healthy communities of Jesus for the long haul." - **Kelly Bean**, Executive Director, African Road, co-planter Urban Abbey, co-founder Convergence, author of *How to Be a Christian Without Going to Church: The Unofficial Guide to Alternative Christian Community.*

"Community not individualism, shared life in proximity together—these are the concepts that grabbed my imagination as I read Mark Votava's book *The Communal Imagination.* Weaving his personal story with the wisdom he has gained from rooting himself in a community that has become home, workplace and worship space, Mark engages us in a journey of discovery and revelation. His practice-based experiences of sacredness in the ordinary and how it opens us up to being the body of Christ is both compelling and refreshing. Think global, act local gains new meaning through this book." -- **Christine Sine**, Executive Director, Mustard Seed Associates.

The Communal Imagination

May your journey
into community
bring great discovery
and peace.

[signature]

The Communal Imagination

Finding a Way to Share
Life Together

MARK VOTAVA

Urban Loft Publishers | Portland, Oregon

The Communal Imagination
Finding a Way to Share Life Together

Urban Loft Publishers
2034 NE 40th Avenue #414
Portland, OR 97212
www.theurbanloft.org

ISBN-13: 978-1495487422
ISBN-10: 1495487423

Made in the U.S.A.

Cover design by Justin Crockett

Table of Contents

Foreword
by Paul Sparks

Over the past 25 years of ministry life I have attended dozens of conferences, heard hundreds of speakers, and read thousands of books that have taught how people can develop imagination by intersecting with new people, new perspectives and new places. And this advice is true and important. New imagination can be catalyzed at the intersection of the new and different. But this author fosters a very different and subversive approach to the subject of imagination. I have known Mark for nearly 15 years, and while Mark travels to new places, visits various faith communities, and reads new books—much of Mark's life is filled with practices that would seem least likely to fire this world-shaking imagination.

In this book you will hear pieces of Mark's ordinary extraordinary life (one in which I have had the honor of being part of for some time). Throughout the years of longing for and living into community in the neighborhood he has opted out of traditional visions of "success" and chosen menial jobs that allowed him to practice deeper presence in the neighborhood. He has worked as a dishwasher, a maintenance hand, a parking attendant, and now as a member of the Catholic Worker (a group in our parish that lives with and on behalf of the poor and marginalized). Many of his days are comprised of meeting with people others pay no attention to, helping out with the hopes and dreams of various friends and neighbors, or quietly contemplating how to grow in love and kindness. I have not been to many conferences on imagination or innovation that advocated this. No one has said, "Just stick out it with your neighbors ... just enter into the ordinary ... just commit to being present in the neighborhood, and your imagination will be ignited like never before."

For thousands of years most of the world has lived in communal settings, close to the land, and connected to the customs and culture of the very particular place they lived in. The issues were exclusion, insularity, and control—but community was never in question. It is only in the last two hundred years that the Western world has made a massive exit from the responsibilities of place, from the ties of community, and from the limitations of the human body. What began as a means of escaping the insularity of village life, the blind patriarchy and dictatorial rule of so many chiefs, rulers, and priests, has turned into a full-on escape from our true interdependence and a shared life in community.

The imagination can be a medium for entering into life fully or it can be a vehicle of escape—escape from truth, escape from commitment, and escape from faithful relationships. Both the Industrial Revolution and the Information Revolution witnessed an explosion of invention, innovation, and creativity unparalleled in history. But, in the name of progress, we have often sacrificed the slow and life-giving imagination that is grown throughout the course of neighborly relations fostered over the course of time. This is an imagination that is developed through years of walking the same streets, plowing the same ground, working the same craft, creating the stronger and stronger fabric of love and care for the stranger, the outsider and the immigrant.

While the main version we have been trained to adopt in the Western world is one of extreme individualism and living above place, there is a growing sub-version. It cannot be discovered by our traditional measurements. But if we take time to unplug from the media, walk outside our insulated buildings, and foster a communal imagination in ordinary neighborhood life, we will discover that the Spirit is already at work and waiting for us to join in.

The Communal Imagination grows the capacity for entering fully into relational life. Years of patient study, prayerful contemplation, and slow relationships developed over the course of time in place, have awakened Mark to the hidden revelations that can only be discovered on the other side of the new, the trendy, the fast, and the entertaining. Instead of an imagination of escape, this is a book that enables a communal imagination. This is an imagination that transforms the ordinary into sacred, that enables faithful relational bonds of love and care, that grows the reciprocal care that causes the land to flourish, and fully embraces the boundaries of our bodies in all of their finitude.

This book reminds me of life together in place. It is filled with seemingly ordinary stories that surprise us with their beauty. The pages shed tears of raw honesty and painful vulnerability. The sections are thick with hidden treasures that hide themselves from the fast consumer. Like the parish, this book is best read devotionally, habitually, prayerfully, slowly, and in meaningful engagement with others.

Paul Sparks, is the co-founding director of the Parish Collective (www.parishcollective.org) and author of *The New Parish: How Neighborhood Churches Are Transforming Mission, Discipleship and Community.*

Foreword

Part 1

Developing the Context: Where We Start

Chapter 1

Life Together: The Context for a Culture of
Imagination

I have always struggled with the relational contexts that I have lived in. The family I was born into, my cultural context, and my religious experiences all left me with an overwhelming desire to run away, to escape from it all. Struggle has characterized my life for so long that I have often wanted to leave these contexts altogether. You see, I didn't just learn individualism from my educational and entertainment experiences: This was the coping mechanism I learned as a matter of survival for the first three decades of my life.

The family situation I was raised in, my mom and dad plus five sisters and one brother, was often difficult for me. My parents did love me in their own way, but rarely did I experience a lot of love in a way that connected with me as a young kid. Sometimes it got so bad that I wanted to deny my family upbringing, even though this is where I came from. The members of my family had a hard time getting along with one another, as many families often do. It was common for my parents to fight and yell at each other, and I did not want to be around them very much as I got older. My mom would often threaten to leave after a fight with my dad.

We lived in a three-bedroom little rambler house with only one bathroom. We were poor and my dad often had to work two or three jobs just to pay for basics like food and utilities. I became ashamed of my upbringing. Sometimes, the tension was so bad that I didn't know what to do. As this tension grew over the years, the desire to leave my family and never speak to them again had crossed my mind many times. Sometimes, even still, I find myself angry at God for the kind of family I was born into. Why couldn't I be from a more supportive, loving family who valued me the way I am? Why couldn't we all just get along together?

Growing up in the United States has not been easy for me either. I felt suffocated by the culture's expectations for me to be popular and successful. The pressure to find my identity in money, possessions and a prestigious career left me disillusioned. I grew up in the Pacific Northwest during the time of the grunge music scene. I could always identify with bands like Nirvana who struggled under the pressure to measure up to something they did not value very much, to be somebody they were not.

I was left disillusioned with the unbalanced individualism that characterizes so much of the Western world. Over the course of time, though, I began to realize that running away from it all may not be the best option (although sometimes I still feel like it). Instead, I have had to learn to face this situation with a new imagination for engaging life where I am.

Living within the constraints of popular culture has been one of the hardest experiences of my life, because it constantly promotes an individualism without interdependence. This always left me feeling disconnected, fragmented and lonely. Many times I have wanted to leave my cultural context and move out of the country altogether. Sometimes I think this will bring me to a better place where many of my problems will disappear and life will be much easier. But I know that this isn't true. Leaving my life will only cause me to face my challenges somewhere else. Pain and difficulty will not just disappear by leaving where I come from.

My experiences with religion and the Church have not left me faring much better. It always seemed that the people I encountered were not truly relational and authentic. The churches and cathedrals I encountered promoted an individualistic spirituality that did not always support interdependence in everyday life. They seemed to offer services, but I was looking for deep friendship and relational meaning. Their projects and propositions were frustrating for me, an ordinary guy who needed meaningful connection in everyday life with others. Consequently, I have rarely fit in with churches that felt like an institution. And yet staying connected to people of faith is what God has been calling me to do. Living in anger or cynicism will not do. But pretending that I am happy about the ways I have experienced my Christianity has not been helpful either. It is so much easier to give up on the Church than to have an imagination for something more.

I am coming to understand that I cannot completely abandon the relational contexts that I live in. There may be times that I must leave those contexts in order for God to teach and awaken me, but I am discovering that the Spirit uses the people and places to which we are called to transform our lives and give us hope. I can no longer abandon my sense of responsibility to where God has placed me. I have discovered that the Spirit gives me strength and support to make decisions that can bring life and healing. God has used my struggle of place to give me courage and love. I can no longer use my human agency to lead a selfish lifestyle detached from my relational context. All my experiences have helped me realize that the reality of friendship, family, and community is a miracle that requires divine grace, both if we're to live together faithfully, and to respond with loving courage when we don't.

After all of these years of pain and struggle, I am now realizing that developing a way of sanity in the middle of the craziness I was born into requires nurturing an alternative imagination with others who long for a life rooted in God. Throughout the rest of this writing, I will explore some practices we have discovered for cultivating a culture of imagination together in everyday life. This will move us to a more life-giving way of being the body of Christ in our fragmented culture.

Subverting the Mindset of Individualism: Learning Interdependence

Sometimes the right story can really transform the imagination. I'll never forget going into our little neighborhood cinema in Downtown Tacoma and seeing the film *Into the Wild*. It is a true story about a young man by the name of Christopher McCandless, who experiences disillusionment with the dreams promoted by his family and schooling in Western culture. He realizes the deep brokenness behind the facade of what society often deems as success. After giving away the money he had saved for law school, he went on a journey to live in the Alaskan wilderness with almost nothing but his will to discover life, freedom, and truth.

Christopher encounters all kinds of new friends on his journey from Georgia to Alaska, but leaves them all in pursuit of his dream to flee society and live in the wild. He loves the books of Tolstoy, London, and Thoreau; he delights in their rugged individualism, and their rejection of mainstream success. He has only one thing on his mind throughout his travels: to get to Alaska and experience life the way it was meant to be, in its purest form, with nothing but the rivers, sky, fresh air, and trees around him. It takes him about two years, but he finally manages to get to Alaska.

After several months of living in an abandoned bus in the middle of the Alaskan wilderness, he cannot find any more animals to hunt. There is a scene where he is screaming about how hungry he is out under the open sky. Desperate, he searches out berries to pick and eat. But the next day he awakens to a growing pain in his stomach and realizes that he has eaten berries that were poisonous. If left untreated, his digestive tract will stop functioning, and he'll starve to death. Trapped in the wilderness because the river is too high for him to cross back over, he cannot get back to civilization and get help.

In a very moving closing scene, he realizes what has happened and breaks down and weeps. He knows he is going to die alone in the wild with no one to help him, or even someone to share his pain. His body is weak to the point where he can barely move. With his last efforts he scratches into his journal a final untimely revelation: Life is only to be experienced when it is shared. Soon afterwards he lies down on the mattress in the bus with his head looking into the sky, takes his last breath, and dies.

As I left the theatre, I could not shake its powerful, and even disturbing hold on me. What life, beauty and potential there was in this young man. His imagination and hope for another way of life was so powerful that it was able to shake him out of cultural complacency. But what a disturbing conclusion! In escaping the traps of culture, he lost the hope that is found in relationships. He needed others in his life. Individual pursuits, no matter how worthy, could only take him so far. Disconnection and isolation from others not only wore upon his spirit; in the end, it took his life.

I remember walking out of the movie theatre shocked and saddened that such a promising life could end in such a tragic way. But we do this same kind of thing all the time, using different techniques to keep from having to live interdependently with others. Shane Claiborne says in his book *The Irresistible Revolution*, "Community is what we were created for ... But that doesn't mean community is easy. For everything in this world tries to pull us away from community, pushes us to choose independence over interdependence, to choose great things over small things, to choose going fast alone over going far together."[1]

We have been raised in a culture that prizes independence, and most of us are unconsciously trained as children to think of it as the good,

---

[1] Claiborne, *The Irresistible Revolution*, 134-135.

Christian, American way. But this individualistic way of life has been taken to the far extreme, and it is killing our imaginations. We are biologically constituted for interdependence and shared life. We do not make our own lives, but we allow others to influence and be influenced by us. Extreme individualism is not healthy for a person, let alone an entire culture. It is like we are eating poisonous berries not knowing that we will soon die.

In a culture that values the individualistic over the interdependent, we become disconnected from one another. I have suffered from my own programming toward individualism and have longed to be set free to live into something different. I'm haunted by these words of Christ: "For whoever wants to save his live will lose it, but whoever loses his life for me and for the gospel will save it" (Mark 8:35). I want to understand what this means and how to embody Christ's words. Can we lose our individualistic dreams and ambitions that take priority over everything and everyone else? Can we stop the pain that is caused by our self-centered pursuits where the imagination necessary for relational life is forgotten?

It's one thing to disconnect ourselves from the cultural comfort of the modern paradigm of success, but the authentic life should not be lived alone. Our imaginations are coming to the point of starvation and death. We must develop an imagination for interdependence and loving mutuality, if we are to flourish together. All the systems of our culture are ripping us away from one another, and few of us have awakened to what is happening. Our imaginations need the shared experience of life, goodness, and beauty. We cannot know for sure what will happen in us and through us together, but I think it will be something beautiful as we let go of all our controlling individualistic ways of life.

We can't let our imaginations be captivated by the "normal" individualistic agenda of the twenty-first century. Brian J. Walsh and Sylvia C. Keesmaat make it clear that this type of "normal" is not necessarily good. "The primary way any imperial culture claims our lives is through the captivity of our imaginations. Take an average of twenty-six hours of television a week, thousands of brand-name logos a day, an education system structured to produce law-abiding consumers who always crave more, and dress it all up with a mythology of divine right to world rule, and it is not surprising that the dominant worldview is so deeply internalized in the population – including the church – that it is simply taken to be the only viable, normal and commonsensical way of life."[2] When you've been raised like this it seems so much like common sense, but it really makes no sense at all.

My friend Mark Scandrette, the Executive Director of *Reimagine,* a center for spiritual formation in San Francisco's Mission District neighborhood, claims that "our interconnectedness should seem obvious – except for the fact that many of us have been groomed by a society that celebrates the success of the individual apart from the community."[3] We need more prophets of local, relational living within the body of Christ who will inspire our imaginations toward a more relational way of life together within a particular place.

The ways of individualism need to be subverted. The ways of interdependence need to be liberated and celebrated in our day and age. The mental illness of this disease of individualism is corroding our humanity into something that is ugly and mutilated. It is not natural or right to dismember the body of Christ this way. The local church should be the most interdependent, caring fabric of relationships around. We have frightfully let our days fill up with things that do not promote togetherness. We do not relate to each other on a daily basis in ways that foster life, reconciliation and hope. How long will we live this way and destroy our relational imaginations of generosity, compassion, care, and hospitality toward one another? If we could get back to interdependence with one another in life, we would live more wholly.

---

2 Walsch and Keesmaat, *Colossians Remixed,* 176.

3 Scandrette, *Soul Graffiti,* 50.

Being and Becoming the Local Body: Fitting Together in Everyday Life

Through a lifetime of spiritual searching, Catholic mystic Thomas Merton came to the conclusion that, "We all need one another, we all complete one another. God's will is found in this mutual interdependence."[4] What a profound statement! Christians today need to recover this basic relational connection with one another in daily life. This is necessary if we are to find God's will, and manifest any sort of goodness and beauty in life together. As we practice being and becoming a local body that fits together in everyday life, that place will form the context for guiding and releasing a *Culture of Imagination*. It will begin to subvert the individualistic techniques we try to hide behind.

You can see how this works when you read the Scriptures as though they were addressing a tangible local body instead of an individual. The Scriptures were not written primarily to an individual, but to a collective of people who were learning to embody the gospel in everyday life. The apostle Paul wrote to the local church in Corinth to remind them:

> By means of his one Spirit, we all said goodbye to our partial and piecemeal lives. We each used to independently call all our own shots, but then we entered into a large and integrated life in which he has the final say in everything. ... The old labels we once used to identify ourselves—labels like Jew or Greek, slave or free—are no longer useful. We need something larger, more comprehensive (1 Corinthians 12:13,14 *The Message*).

It was always a *We*–thing, not an *I*-thing. The *I* is important to the *We*, but cannot stand alone. Often we turn our spirituality into an I-thing where it is all about "me and God." This epidemic of isolation and loneliness is a disease that needs to be dealt with. Michael Frost reminds us in his book *Jesus the Fool*,

---

[4] Merton, *Life and Holiness*, 38.

We have become a culture of individualists, all calling for our rights at the expense of others. The result is that our societies have become inevitably fractured. Whenever a strong individualism is not balanced by a commitment to companionship then isolation and fragmentation become the order of the day. The real disabilities in our culture, as in Christ's, are human isolation and a sense of rejection from one's environment. The reality is that we can never be completely whole in and of ourselves. We need others to make our lives complete. Did you hear that? We need each other. There is a point beyond which our sense of self-determination becomes inaccurate, arrogant, and increasingly self-defeating … We are inevitably social creatures who desperately need each other not merely for sustenance or for company but for any meaning to our lives whatsoever.[5]

Frost calls our isolation from one another a disability. Are we all living with disabilities and mental illnesses due to our individualistic ways of life that only give lip service to the body of Christ in everyday life? Connecting with other people gives our lives meaning. Friendships are the most important investments we can make. We need to give our lives to one another and be the body of Christ together. Can we be connected as friends together on a daily basis? All of life is relational and it is the relational that gives substance to all that we are as human beings in the world. What matters most is everyday life in the place that we live.

How can we be the body of Christ together in the day-to-day of life despite the individualism, fragmentation, and loneliness we all experience at times? I have experienced many years of trying to be connected to people of faith who have no commitment to one another, or to the place where they live. It has been frustrating. Many times I have wanted to give up because it seems that all of our spirituality is lived out of a Western individualistic paradigm. But I want to encourage others not to give up. There is another path to a way of interdependence within the body of Christ in everyday life. And it

---

[5] Frost, *Jesus the Fool,* 151-152.

seems that there is a slow turning towards a Culture of Imagination that God intended from the beginning of creation.

I have often asked myself the question, "What is life about?" I don't know a lot of the time, but I am discovering that I need an interdependence with others to even open up the question. This cannot be discovered in isolation from others. The context of my relationships in the place that I live is the medium that helps me to discern what life is and who I am. I must resist the temptation to run away when the relational revelations come at me too strongly and I lack the courage to face them. These situations have the power to break down my arrogance and help me rely on God in order to live into my context with more authenticity and imagination.

William Shannon says, "Accepting the truth of my existence means accepting the relationships that life brings to me and realizing that these relationships are also gifts: gifts that come to me because I live in a particular time and place. I do not exist in isolation, but in a series of interlocking relationships which, like the gifts I possess, play a necessary role in my achieving and discovering who I am as a person. Relationships may be crippling or they may be life-sustaining. They may hinder growth or enhance it. If they are wholesome gifts, they build up community where there is a blossoming of gifts and a nurturing of life."[6]

The interdependent life is like a garden of vegetables or flowers that grow to produce life-sustaining substance and beauty for everyday life. What would life be like without such things? We would not be very healthy and some aspects of beauty would never be realized. I hope we all set out on a path of discovery to find a healthier, beautiful life together in everyday life.

---

[6] Shannon, *Silence on Fire*, 92.

Creating the Context: Commitment to Place, Locality, and
Neighborhood

To even start the process of shared life together in everyday life there
needs to be a radical reorientation towards a commitment to a
particular place. The body of Christ needs to see itself as a fabric of
relationships living, working, and playing within the proximity of a local
context. In other words, we have to practice inhabiting a neighborhood
and committing to that place as the body of Christ together.

Reimagining the local body of Christ this way breaks open the
paradigm of the regional commuter church that is disconnected in
everyday life and then meets inside the four walls of a building we
culturally call "church." This is the only paradigm most of us have ever
known. But is the body of Christ supposed to be confined to such a
limiting imagination? So many people have given up on the body of
Christ simply because the mediums we have created communicate that
Christianity has nothing to do with the realities of everyday life. Put
bluntly, it is irrelevant. Most of the time, we only care about the things
that actually affect our individual lives. These are the things we invest
our lives in, because we feel it will give us life with the most pleasure,
enjoyment and meaning. That's why the mediums we have created as
"the expression of the body of Christ" do not seem relevant. They
communicate vibes of boredom and unpleasantness. I have struggled
with these mediums myself and my faith has had a hard time surviving
through a default that produces a lack of engagement in real life.

What I want to propose is that the body of Christ reorient around the
themes of *community* and *parish* (that is, contextual to neighborhood
and local culture).

There are many ideas and definitions of community today that spring
from affinity groups, city associations and the conversations of the
emerging and missional Church, but I like Wendell Berry's definition:
"If the word community is to mean or amount to anything, it must refer
to a place (in its natural integrity) and its people. It must refer to a

placed people."[7] Berry goes on to say, "It exists by proximity, by neighborhood; it knows face to face, and it trusts as it knows…"[8] Proximity is crucial to this definition of community. Without it there is no community. This has to be taken seriously and then practiced together if there is to be any real face-to-face interaction as the body of Christ in everyday life. The neighborhood cannot be forgotten. I believe that the neighborhood or parish is the holistic medium that we need if we are to live into a healthy expression of the body of Christ that does not do damage to its local context.

"Here is the mystery of the incarnation," says Gerald W. Schlabach. "Union of human and divine means that faith always must express itself in specific, local, particular ways."[9] The incarnation is one of the foundational theological doctrines of Christianity. Yet why is it that the incarnation has often been disconnected from our own practice as the body of Christ? I think it is because the only expression of the church that we know is what goes on inside a building. The building is not the church, but without the body of Christ having a commitment to shared life in a particular place there is nothing but the building. This medium of the building communicates that the incarnation has no relevance to the particulars of everyday life in a local context together. There is a big disconnect between the building and the local cultural context of a neighborhood.

Just as the building is not the church, so also abstract words do not comprise the whole of the gospel. We need to approach the neighborhood as a listener and learner and be careful with the abstract words we speak. The gospel cannot be communicated fully if it is not the embodiment of love and care. The gospel is love; it is more than words and empty gestures. How can we love as the body of Christ if we are rootless and without commitment to people in real life? It just doesn't work and finds itself once again irrelevant.

---

[7] Berry, *Sex, Economy, Freedom and Community*, 168.

[8] Ibid., 161.

[9] Schlabach, *Unlearning Protestantism*, 106.

The Gospel of John (1:14) reminds us that "The Word became flesh and made his dwelling among us." Or as *The Message* says, "The Word became flesh and blood, and moved into the neighborhood." Christ is the Word who became human and lived in a particular local context that shaped him all throughout his life. The place he lived shaped who he became as a person. It was the context God used to speak to him.

Jesus did not try to escape his responsibilities and relationships, but embraced them. He learned to love and care for his neighbors. Most of the people couldn't believe he was the Son of God because he was so ordinary and familiar. How could he be the Son of God? No way! But the incarnation calls us to live our faith together in our local context just as Christ did in his life. There cannot be a disconnection within the body of Christ regarding the incarnation. Michael Frost and Alan Hirsch make this clear in their book *The Shaping of Things to Come*. It is worth quoting extensively.

> It has been said, "If we want to make a thing real we must make it local." That is precisely what God did in Jesus Christ – the divine love took on a local habitation and a name. The coming of God among us was not just a momentary theophany, but constituted an actual 'dwelling' among us... In the light of such a dwelling, place—geography itself—took on a sacred meaning. He became known as Jesus of Nazareth. It is interesting to ponder whether Nazareth itself, a poor town in ancient Israel, actually had a role in the formation of Jesus... To be theologically true to the meaning of the humanity of Jesus, we have to recognize that Jesus was who he was, not only because he was God, but because he was formed through his real engagement with his social milieu. As an authentic human being, Jesus was Jesus precisely because of Mary and Joseph, his twelve disciples, the poor to whom he ministered, and all the others who interacted with him in the myriad ways common to human life. He was changed in some way by all those he came in contact with in precisely the same way that we are changed by our relationships – for good or ill. To be a genuine human being, Jesus must have had such relational encounters .[10]

---

[10] Frost and Hirsch, *The Shaping of Things to Come*, 36.

A commitment to a particular place embeds us in continual relational encounters where we have to learn to love each other as the body of Christ. It is also the crucible for learning to love our neighbors. The neighborhood holds us all together and teaches us how to live with potential differences of personality, gender, race, and class.

The reality of life is that we are all different. Even followers of Christ tend to be very different. We need to find a way to live together in everyday life and not run from our differences. A commitment to the local context can help us to see others more empathetically. Living life together helps people collaborate together around their differences. It also helps people discover what they have in common. Without having a common commitment to the geographic proximity of a place, you end up with many "churches" but no functioning body in everyday life. This movement toward shared life in the parish may be a hard transition for people to make together, but it is so necessary.

Making the Transition: The Journey into Parish

My own experience has been a difficult one. I have been a part of a ministry called The Downtown Neighborhood Fellowship for the past ten years or so. When I first began attending some of the meetings, it was a college-age outreach with hundreds of people, and a different name. It was a big social environment with alternative music, innovative and exciting speakers, and people attending from all over the region. It was actually a pretty good expression of some of the emerging ideas of the time. But my close friend Paul Sparks, who was the founder of the outreach, was beginning to feel a disconnection from the lives of everyday people. It felt like it was becoming a big event with disparate people, who experienced very little transformation, very little true friendship, and very little care for other people.

In an effort to reconnect relationally we started a leadership school that focused on listening to one another and learning from our context. Hundreds of people went through the school and our experiences together brought many of us to a point of re-evaluating our purpose together. After a lot of school sessions and several internships, we came to the point where we told everyone that if they wanted to be involved it would require them to reorient their lives around the neighborhood of Downtown Tacoma. Many people left and ultimately, we ended up with about ten leaders who wanted to live within the proximity of the neighborhood.

We were embarrassed by how we handled the transition because of our inexperience, but also because it felt like we had just unraveled the whole ministry. But slowly, over the years, we began to integrate into the neighborhood, with a listening posture of being shaped by the very context we were living in. We were criticized by others of faith who thought that we had ruined a good thing, but we were welcomed by the people in the neighborhood who saw that we wanted to learn from them, share life with them, and genuinely cared to listen to their lives. It's kind of a backwards story. We learned to be a better witness to the gospel by not saying too much too early, and learning to live relationally in a place, caring for the local context of a neighborhood.

To this day our fellowship struggles with the question, "How can our lives together become less fragmented and more holistic?" Our society promotes a lifestyle of fragmentation where we go here to do this, we go somewhere else to do that. There are so many things and people to be involved with all over the place, whether in different cities, or in different neighborhoods within the same city. Our minds are spinning in confusion and at times we border on insanity. For us, regaining some peace has meant learning to stop and center our lives within a commitment to the parish. Our transition toward neighborhood has been difficult, but the rest and the authenticity we now experience have been worth it.

Each person's journey back into place will be different. But we need to get reconnected with a place, a local context to inhabit as the body of Christ in our day. As Alan J. Roxburgh says, "We discover what God is doing in the world and what it means to be the church as we move back into the neighborhood. This is both a simple and radical proposal. It's radical because for many of us there is little connection between where we live ... and what it means to be a Christian. That's the tragic state of Christian life in North America ... A radical way we can re-form Christian life in our time is by the simple decision to reconnect with our neighborhoods, by asking what God is doing there."[11]

The neighborhood has an unceasing number of relational revelations to teach us if we are ready to listen. God has been working and manifesting himself in particular places for centuries. That is where relational, holistic ways of living take place. Some people want to care for a large city or region—perhaps even a country—but when it comes to relationships of care, these are all too big. The neighborhood is large enough to live life together, but not so big that there is a relational disconnection due to an overwhelming number of people and places. Tim Dickau in his fascinating book *Plunging Into The Kingdom Way* gets after this problem: "If you work in one place, shop in another, play in a third and 'go to church' (which is bad theology to begin with) in a fourth, life becomes more fragmented. When you are part of a community that inhabits a neighborhood with a vision to be involved in its transformation, life itself becomes more integrated and whole. Our communities become kinder, and we begin to consider each other's welfare as we make economic, social, and political decisions."[12]

In the Scriptures it is just assumed that people lived in their local context because they didn't have the technology and mobility that we have today. Unfortunately, we do not have very many Bible verses that talk about becoming rooted in a place and committing to a local culture, because that's just how everyone naturally lived. Our technological culture has taught us to escape being the body of Christ together in everyday life because we can. We feel we are wiser for doing so, but I don't think we are. We feel we can achieve more, be more, and love more people without being committed to a place. We have been

---

[11] Roxburgh, *Missional*, 168.

[12] Dickau, *Plunging into the Kingdom Way*, 12.

convinced that this is the way to live, witnessing to the gospel in all kinds of ways except within the context of a local culture. What a mistake we are making! The gospel cannot be lived except in the particulars of a local context. We cannot love together faithfully except in the particulars of a local context. We cannot even know God relationally except within the particulars of a local context. Loving others and loving God are intertwined into one seamless reality. We cannot have one without the other.

I like the story Jesus tells about the parable of the sower:

> A farmer went out to sow his seed. As he was scattering the seed, some fell along the path, and the birds came and ate it up. Some fell on rocky places, where it did not have much soil. It sprang up quickly, because the soil was shallow. But when the sun came up, the plants were scorched, and they withered because they had no root. Other seed fell among thorns, which grew up and choked the plants. Still other seed fell on good soil, where it produced a crop—a hundred, sixty or thirty times what was sown. He who has ears, let him hear ...

> Listen then to what the parable of the sower means: When anyone hears the message about the kingdom and does not understand it, the evil one comes and snatches away what was sown in his heart. This is the seed sown along the path. The one who received the seed that fell on rocky places is the man who hears the word and at once receives it with joy. But since he has no root, he lasts only a short time. When trouble or persecution comes because of the word, he quickly falls away. The ones who received the seed that fell among the thorns is the man who hears the word, but the worries of this life and the deceitfulness of wealth choke it, making it unfruitful. But the one who received the seed that fell on good soil is the man who hears the word and understands it. He produces a crop, yielding a hundred, sixty or thirty times what was sown (Matthew 13:3-9, 18-23).

I always had the idea when I read this parable that the seeds being scattered by the farmer represented hearing a verbal presentation of the gospel and believing some propositional statements about Christ, thus accepting Christ and making a decision to a more ethical or moral life; one where I start to attend a church building and develop a personal relationship with Christ through the Scriptures. I then begin to hang out with a lot of like-minded people that seem pretty nice. The rest of life, other than the few meetings a week I attend or the ministries I get involved in (service projects), I'm on my own to figure out by myself. I have always been confused and disillusioned by this approach. It seemed there had to be a lot more to the body of Christ then this.

I am coming to a new understanding of what these seeds might mean. Maybe the seeds of the sower are not primarily representative of propositional gospel presentations, but of God's quiet revelations that are spread all around us in everyday life waiting to take root. These revelations reveal God's relational character and guide us toward the life of faithful presence with the Spirit and with one another. The different soils in the parable represent how we respond to these revelations. The seeds need to fall on soil that is open and receptive for the gospel to be embodied and flourish as we commit ourselves over time. I believe the "good soil" is the one who understands the gospel and produces a crop that yields many times more than what was sown. The seeds that fall on the path could represent not committing to faithfulness in your relationships with the people and the place God has called you. Perhaps the soil is not receptive to God because of a fear that "this will limit my options and take away my freedom." But what we don't understand is that this could be our greatest liberation. The seeds that fall on the rocky soil could represent the one who starts on the path of commitment, but because of pride and independence it becomes too difficult relationally to continue. Perhaps this person doesn't give themselves enough time to reconcile with others or the place they live in. Maybe the conflict of everyday life causes them to get weary and leave without relying on God. The seeds that falls on the thorns could be the worries of life that are so common to our culture: finances, marriage, family, careers, possessions, health, what people might think, safety, and comfort. But what we don't realize is that God gives us the courage to be the body of Christ in everyday life and will provide for us what is essential for life together if we will trust him. He only needs us to be receptive to the seeds of revelation and strength. This soil-and-the-seed story could revolutionize the way we are the body of Christ in everyday life together if we have the imagination for it.

Practicing life within the local context of neighborhood is not the easy way, but it is a beautiful way to develop a Culture of Imagination. There are not many models to look at in this day and age regarding how to be the body of Christ together in everyday life. We need bold experiments of trust, love and commitment. When we step into these experiments, in deep reliance on the Spirit, allowing this process of discovery to shape our imaginations for local expression, miracles can happen. If we don't, Tim Keel suggests, "The loss of connection between churches and neighborhoods creates a corresponding loss of localized imagination and creates an addictive-like dependence on acontextual experts."[13]

---

[13] Keel, *Intuitive Leadership*, 75.

Life Together

Chapter 2

The Gift of the Ordinary: Understanding and Embodying Proximity

Weaving the Fabric of Care: A Web of Relationships Lived in Proximity

For quite some time our group, Downtown Neighborhood Fellowship, had been struggling with the question, "What is the church? Is it a building or is it the people?" Most would say it is the people. But if you ask them, "Where is the church on Monday (or any other day of the week apart from Sunday)," they will point to the building. This happens because there is usually very little expression of the body of Christ in everyday life. Once our fellowship began to imagine the local church as the people instead of the building, we knew we had to become a fabric of relationships lived within the proximity of a local context in everyday life. We knew we had to live with the relational purpose of being present, expressing love, listening closely and collaborating together. This presence--loving, listening and collaborating--doesn't just mean living relationally with people in the local context; it also means living relationally with God. God becomes a subject of discovery through the relational context of the neighborhood.

I keep asking that the God of our Lord Jesus Christ, the glorious Father, may give you the Spirit of wisdom and revelation, so that you may know him better. I pray also that the eyes of your heart will be enlightened in order that you may know the hope to which he has called you, the riches of his glorious inheritance in the saints, and his incomparably great power for us who believe. That power is like the working of his mighty strength, which he exerted in Christ when he raised him from the dead and seated him at his right hand in the heavenly realms, far above all rule and authority, power and dominion, and every title that can be given, not only in the present age but also in the one to come. And God placed all things under his feet and appointed him to be head over everything for the church, which is his body, the fullness of him who fills everything in every way (Ephesians 1:17-23).

Paul wrote this to the believers in Ephesus to encourage the body of Christ to live out the gospel where they were. The relational context always invites wisdom, revelation and enlightenment. If Christ's power is made manifest to his church, which is the people in the context of a place, then the network of relationships within the neighborhood will soon begin to be shaped by relational revelations of deep wisdom and enlightenment. Christ will begin to live out his life within his body on earth as we share life together throughout each day, week, season and year of our lives. Whether fall, winter, spring or summer, Christ's enlightenment through our relationships in the place that we inhabit will continue to grow in our lives.

We need to be the church, the body of Christ in everyday life. We are together his hands and feet every day of the week. For the first three hundred years after Christ was crucified and resurrected, the local body of Christ was a web of relationships living in a place, learning to show hospitality and compassion to all. They probably never even thought in paradigms of "going to church." It would have probably sounded strange to them. They saw themselves as the church, the body of Christ. They didn't see the church as an institution or a building. As missiologist Eddie Gibbs states, "In the first three centuries of the church the emphasis was not on going to church but on being the church. The church is not a building or an institution but a body to which one belongs."[1]

I often wonder what it would be like to be around those Christians in the book of Acts. They were real flesh-and-blood people like us who saw a sacredness in their life together as followers of Christ. They needed one another. They cared for one another. They trusted one another. They were in relationship with one another. They probably didn't see this as radical; it was just how they lived as Christ's body together. "Every day they continued to meet together ... They broke bread in their homes and ate together with glad and sincere hearts." (Acts 2:46).

As Christianity started to become institutionalized and the idea of just going to a service became more common, some followers of Christ went out into the desert to create new communities where they could live their faith together in everyday life. This is how monasticism started. They wanted to seek God in the solitude of the desert apart from the over-institutionalization that they felt was corrupting the body of Christ. All of this happened a long time ago. But how will we respond to the institutionalization of the body of Christ in our time? Will we give up and let our imaginations be imprisoned by all of this or will we live relationally with one another, rooted in local contexts within neighborhoods?

The body of Christ is not some mechanism with no heart and life, but a living breathing body. All bodies breathe, move, change and relate to their environment. When bodies are unhealthy they stop functioning properly. When bodies are dead we bury them. Kester Brewin says, "We must reestablish ourselves as the body of Christ, not the machine of Christ. Bodies are organic, dynamic, sentient, and conscious ... Machines break down, while bodies evolve."[2] We should be an evolving

---

[1] Gibbs, *Leadership Next*, 79.

[2] Brewin, *Signs of Emergence*, 85.

body in everyday life together. Will we feel the pain and the joy of living life together and loving one another?

These are difficult real-life experiences that we cannot escape if we are to be human. We are not building a machine but a body. I don't want to become a part of a machine where I become the very fuel that it needs to work. This reminds me of the movie *The Matrix* where Neo finds out that the machine world is using human beings as fuel. Everyone thinks they are living life the way it was meant to be, and no one realizes they are living an illusion. It may be an extreme metaphor but the church of our day seems to be playing inside of a Matrix of its own, and a lot of people are hiding behind its clichés.

I feel that the lay people, the people who are the ordinary folk, who live common ordinary lives are going to be the future practitioners of the body of Christ in local contexts, living in local neighborhoods, receiving wisdom through experiments of local embodiment. Living relationally, in locality, in neighborhood, doesn't take any fancy theological degrees from prestigious schools to accomplish. All it really takes is a willingness to be faithful to God and to others and to a place. All it takes is a listening posture to change and live your life together with others in community. All it takes is vulnerability and courage. All it takes is investing your life and giving up our extreme individualism and learning how to be the church together. Elaine A. Heath and Scott T. Kisker in their book *Longing for Spring,* say, "The pattern of renewal occurs over and over in the history of the church. Worldliness creeps into the structures of the church, and God inspires His people to experiment with models of faithfulness. Renewal does not happen when the laity 'take control' of the church, but rather when the laity realize we are the church."[3]

Look at the following passages. Each one was written to local expressions of the church encouraging them to live out their faith together:

---

[3] Heath and Kisker, *Longing for Spring,* 37.

The Church of Phillipi: "And this is my prayer: that your love may abound more and more in knowledge and depth of insight, so that you may be able to discern what is best and may be pure and blameless until the day of Christ, filled with the fruit of righteousness that comes through Jesus Christ—to the glory and praise of God." (Philippians 1:9-11).

The Church of Colossae: "We always thank God, the Father of our Lord Jesus Christ, when we pray for you, because we have heard of your faith in Christ Jesus and of the love you have for all the saints – the faith and love that spring from the hope that is stored up for you in heaven and that you have already heard about in the word of truth, the gospel that has come to you." (Colossians 1:3-6).

The Church of Thessalonica: "We always thank God for all of you, mentioning you in our prayers. We continually remember before our God and Father your work produced by faith, your labor prompted by love, and your endurance inspired by hope in our Lord Jesus Christ" (1 Thessalonians 1:2-3).

Did you notice a common trend here? These words would not have been written to these people in particular places if there was no shared life together in proximity. So we can see that the body of Christ in the early church was much more than what we experience today in institutionalized service models. The body of Christ was not treated like a machine but functioned in everyday life. The people who called themselves followers of The Way learned to live the life of Christ in daily relationship with one another and care for their local context. That was the only life they knew.

Receiving God's Grace: The Sacred Gift of Life Together

Are we not all called to share life together to some degree? I think we are. In my neighborhood of Downtown Tacoma, I have come to see a shared life with my friends there as a true gift from God. It is a seed of life that will grow and flourish over time. It is nice to be connected to other people of faith who care for the place we inhabit together. Shared life will sustain us through life. When we have good times, we need friends to celebrate with us. When we have bad times, we need friends to cry with. Life is a mystery and we need to live in relationship with others or we will easily become isolated, disconnected and depressed. The pain we all experience in life will destroy us all if we are not committed to a place, where we live in the context of shared life with friends who care for us as human beings instead of objects.

For years I have studied the life and work of Dorothy Day, the co-founder of the Catholic Worker Movement. After years and years of loving the poor and trying to live in faithful service to God, she shares at the end of her autobiography *The Long Loneliness:* "The only answer in this life, to the loneliness we are all bound to feel, is community. The living together, working together, sharing together, loving God and loving our brother, and living close to him in community so we can show our love for Him."[4]

I have experienced a lot of pain and disconnection in life. My college experience was a common one, I believe, for many of us. Central Washington University is where I chose to study to become a teacher. As I moved to Eastern Washington to a little town called Ellensburg, I did not know very many people there or the place I was moving to. The several years that I lived there, I became connected to the students at the school. Surrounded by lots of people on a daily basis, I had developed many connections with others. It was a sad day for me when I graduated and moved back to Western Washington, because I was pretty much alone again. It seemed like I was starting over. All my relational connections in everyday life were gone. Being uprooted from my college experience and moving on to become a professional left me extremely lonely. After moving to Kent, Washington, where I knew hardly anyone except for some family members, I was out in the world on my own. I was now a professional teacher and I started working for a school district.

---

[4] Day, *The Long Loneliness*, 243.

But I didn't like it very much. It wasn't really what I thought it would be. Monday through Friday I went to work, and mostly stayed in my apartment the rest of the time. Depression and loneliness soon began to overwhelm me as I started to sleep a lot. I was extremely disconnected from relationships with others. After struggling for about a year, I slowly began to see my need to take some initiative in the relationships around me. When I started to open up to relating with others, I began a process of healing within myself. And this has led me to who I am today. For many of us, it seems like college is the closest experience we will ever have of sharing life with others in everyday life. And yet college is very temporary. When it is over, we often feel disconnected and lonely.

In our early years, we all enter a very communal experience through elementary school, if we stay at the same school. We are with the same students all year in the same classroom. There is quite a bit of shared life in the classroom. It is a little different in middle school and high school in that we have many different classes and teachers, but it is still very much an experience of shared life with peers. That's why some people say our high school days are the best days of our lives because most of us will never share life with that many people again the rest of our lives. When those days are over many of us go to college and then get married, work a career, buy a house and often have little connection to any real community life. We are a lonely society that has been disconnected from shared life with others. How sad it all is. But we have tasted little bits of its potential through our years in school. Norman Wirzba points out so elegantly:

> We live in a broken and wounded world and in a culture that encourages isolation and fragmentation. But from a practical standpoint, the desire for wholeness means that we make our local community and habitat, the native network of relationships that directly feed and nurture us, the focus of sustained attention ... This is not so that we can avoid what is foreign, different, or exotic. It is rather so that we can see more clearly and understand with greater honesty the requirements, limits, and potential of our life together. It is so that we can become fully attentive to our concrete situation,

celebrate the gifts that we are to each other, and take responsibility for our collective needs.[5]

Our lives together in everyday life is such a sacred gift. Working, sharing, playing, listening, caring, loving, socializing, laughing, crying, imagining together is a miracle of God. I want to see the miracles of God manifested through my relationships in my neighborhood. The more and more we share life, the more we will be people of deep wisdom in the place we live. "Wisdom calls aloud in the street, she raises her voice in the public squares; at the head of the noisy streets she cries out" (Proverbs 1:20-21). I like how wisdom is calling out in places that are common constructs of a neighborhood: streets and public squares.

My friends and I have shared many moments together over the years. I love my community. I don't know what I would do with them. They give me strength and encouragement. They inspire me and believe in me. They show me love and understanding. They listen to me in my brokenness. They hold my pain. They forgive me when I fail. They guide me when I am confused. They know me.

Sacredness stems from relationship. All things are sacred because all things are relational. God has created humanity in sacredness. Our lives are sacred. Names are sacred. The particulars of life are sacred. Community is sacred. The seasons of life are sacred. The ordinary is sacred. Moments are sacred. Laughter is sacred. Tears are sacred. There is nothing that can escape this sacredness.

It is by grace that God holds our lives together here and now. It is by grace that we can love one another. It is by grace that we can care for a place. It is by grace that we can live in relationship with others. It is by grace that we can work through differences. It is by grace that we can listen. It is by grace that we can be present. And every relational gift of grace we receive from God is a miracle. People might question whether

---

[5] Wirzba, *Living the Sabbath*, 135.

God still does miracles today. I think miracles do still happen every time a Culture of Imagination is embodied in a particular place in everyday life. Jonathan Wilson-Hartgrove in his book *God's Economy* states, "Somehow, by grace, I eventually remember that this whole thing we call community is a gift—that my whole life is a gift—a little glimpse God has given us into the divine economy that never ends. Somehow, I remember this is not about me. It's not even about us. And the great darkness recedes. By a light that's not our own, we find a way to go on together."[6]

Living Into the Ordinary: Opening the Imagination of Everyday Life

Committing to the local parish means committing to the ordinary. The ordinary is where life is lived in a real place with real people. God works through ordinary life, ordinary people, and in ordinary neighborhoods. There is no hype here, only reality. Our shared life together in the place that we live in is only as good as our faithfulness together in the ordinary. The ordinary requires an inspired Culture of Imagination. Without this imagination, the ordinary becomes banal and empty. Michael Frost in his book *Seeing God in the Ordinary* writes, "Here lies the true wisdom: in the belief that in the mundane and the ordinary, the Master's hand is played for all who would have eyes to see it."[7] God is manifesting redemption to the body of Christ through the ordinary. Everyday life is ordinary and oftentimes we don't think it is that important. The ordinary moves slowly and cannot be controlled. But the ordinary will shape us into something extraordinary if we open our imagination to its sacredness.

Seeking God together as the body of Christ often happens within an ordinary local context. Days and nights, weekends and weekdays, fall, winter, spring, summer; all these take place within the ordinary moments and cycles of life. The ordinary is mundane, but the beauty of God can be discovered there. Ronald Rolheiser reminds us that "If God

---

[6] Wilson-Hartgrove, *God's Economy*, 125.

[7] Frost, *Seeing God in the Ordinary*, 39.

is incarnate in ordinary life then we should seek God, first of all, within ordinary life."[8] Jesus was a very ordinary man. If we were alive when he lived in Nazareth and got close to him, we would probably have found him to be very human and ordinary. In fact, I believe a lot of his miracles and parables stemmed out of the ordinary. It was the ordinary people with whom he had ordinary relationships. It was and is very ordinary to be hungry or sick or lonely. Christ always saw the sacredness of the ordinary.

Let's look at the parable of the mustard seed. "The kingdom of heaven is like a mustard seed, which a man took and planted in his field. Though it is the smallest of all your seeds, yet when it grows, it is the largest of garden plants and becomes a tree, so that the birds of the air come and perch in its branches" (Matthew 13: 31-32). In this parable, as in many of his parables, Christ uses what is ordinary to demonstrate what the kingdom of God is like. Here he is referring to such ordinary things as a small mustard seed which turns into a garden plant and then a tree. He is referring to the process of growth when something is planted in a garden and birds perch on tree branches. Seeds, birds, branches, trees and gardens are all very ordinary everyday-life things. Christ doesn't tell us strange religious stories to explain life. He puts everything into the ordinary so that we can relate and understand. Barbara Brown Taylor says, "The most ordinary things are drenched in divine possibilities."[9]

As I have lived in my neighborhood for ten years now, I have seen God work in the ordinary. It is relational. It is slow. It is steady. It is beautiful. It is not religious. It is not what we define as "spiritual." It is not a ministry. It is not a program. It is not a project. It is hard to communicate. But, this is what the body of Christ is called to: life together in the ordinary particulars of a neighborhood. The body of Christ is called to seek God within the ordinary relationships of a place.

---

[8] Rolheiser, *The Holy Longing*, 100.

[9] Taylor, *An Altar in the World*, 201.

This is how we can live in communion with our Creator, with one another, and with the created world around us.

The ordinary will open up our lives to be the body of Christ together in everyday life. The ordinary will heal, nurture, and care for the body in beautiful ways. The ordinary will be our prophetic witness. The ordinary will guide us. The ordinary will teach us to love and show compassion. The ordinary will invite "the real." The ordinary will speak to us. The ordinary will not be manipulated. The ordinary holds wisdom. The ordinary is for the body of Christ what blood is to a human body: Blood fills our human bodies the way the ordinary is to fill the body of Christ. The Holy Spirit is intertwined with the ordinary. If we disregard the ordinary we disregard the church.

I am hesitant to tell my story because it is one of disillusionment and deconstruction. Those terms are not always easy to absorb. But, I am going to tell it anyway, the best I can. I have always felt a strong disconnection in my experience with the church. I have tried and tried but it just seems strange and irrelevant to me, for many of the reasons I have already talked about. I remember when our church first moved to the neighborhood of Downtown Tacoma to try to live out our faith together. I was scared and timid. I didn't know anyone there. What would people think? What would my parents say about me dropping individual opportunities for "success?" But, I wanted to do something that would be both counter-cultural and sustain me as a follower of Christ. So when I moved into Downtown Tacoma in the spring of 2004 it was a risk I took that very few really understood. Our parish was not a very popular place to live. It had lots of abandoned buildings and empty streets. The nights and the weekends were pretty dead and not too many people liked to hang out there. The built environment needed work and there was a lot of poverty. But I believe God gave me an imagination for the place.

I remember walking the streets and questioning myself many times about my decision to move there. One day I woke up with tears in my eyes. I couldn't understand why I was so emotional. Looking back I think I was just weary and lonely. But, as I began to settle there, God planted hopeful possibilities in my imagination. I began asking, "What could this place become?" There were many church buildings and Sunday meeting spaces in Downtown Tacoma, but the body of Christ was hard to find in everyday life. I had to slowly work through my fears, insecurities, loneliness, and pain. I wanted to share life with others in Downtown Tacoma, but it was more difficult than I had thought.

My journey into the ordinary of this place has started to lead me through my pain and disconnection toward love and compassion. Learning and listening to the ordinary has not been easy. I experience a lot of loneliness and pain still, but my imagination is alive and growing and cannot be captivated. Downtown Tacoma is an open book waiting to be written still today. All the stories remain unfinished. The ordinary of this neighborhood is becoming a part of my redemption, salvation and discipleship.

Rooting in Reality: Developing a Practice-Based Theology

> Therefore everyone who hears these words of mine and puts them into practice is like a wise man who built his house on the rock. The rain came down, the streams rose, and the winds blew and beat against that house; yet it did not fall, because it had its foundation on the rock. But everyone who hears these words of mine and does not put them into practice is like a foolish man who built his house on sand. The rain came down, the stream rose, and the winds blew and beat against that house, and it fell with a great crash (Matthew 7:24-27).

It seems that Christ is emphasizing a practice-based approach to life. He must want his body to practice his words and teachings. It is within the context of shared life, proximity, living into the ordinary, seeing the sacredness of life and a commitment to a particular place where the body of Christ can practice their faith as a way of life together. This is very foreign to the dominant paradigms of the day, but Christ's teachings are always based on practical life situations. They are best practiced together in everyday life. The apostle Paul passed this on as well. "Whatever you have learned or received or heard from me, or seen in me—put it into practice." (Philippians 4:9). Or, to the church in Corinth, "Follow my example, as I follow the example of Christ (1 Corinthians 11:1). They must have grown to know Paul deeply and have been encouraged in what they had seen in his relational life among them. He is encouraging them to live with a grounded practice-based theology within their local context just as he did.

We should develop our theology not just from an intellectual or theoretical perspective, but from what I call an "on-the-ground practice-based theology." All theology should be practiced, tested, and even discovered in the context of real-life experience. It should not dismiss everyday life, but instead integrate it with the intellectual stimulation that comes through learning new information. Learning is both intellectual and environmental within the context of the locality we live in. It is not either/or but an integration of both/and. Just as the church cannot be separated from locality, so the academic and intellectual cannot be separated from the environmental and local contexts of life. We desperately need the paradox of combining the environmental learner in local relational contexts with the intellectual academic learner of the classroom. A Christianity that doesn't hold to this paradigm is likely to be empty and irrelevant to life.

Why do many people question the existence of God today? I think it might have something to do with the reality that many people have never seen the body of Christ in the everyday contexts of life. All they have seen is what we box up inside of a building or cram into a ministry one day a week. It doesn't seem holistic to a lot of people—me included. They have not felt from us God's love. They have not experienced from us God's grace. We have not fascinated them with God's beauty.

I think it is important to have an awakening around this on-the-ground practice-based theology. Let's take the theology of the intellectual in the classroom and integrate it with the on-the-ground practice-based theology of the neighborhood. There need not be any dualities between the two. Let them become one and we will see a Culture of Imagination rise from the dead.

A Culture of Imagination needs an on-the-ground practice-based theology to thrive. Our imaginations need the exercise of real-life contexts to grow. They need the practice of living out the teachings of Christ together in the parish. I love these words by Richard Rohr: "We don't think our way into a new life; we live our way into a new kind of thinking."[10] We can't change our way of living by just thinking in new paradigms about theology apart from integrating this with on-the-ground practice-based theology in a local context. Practice and embodiment helps guide our imaginations according to reality. There needs to be an integration between thinking, living and embodiment.

An on-the-ground practice-based theology that is embodied in the local context of everyday life together is the only way that our lives will flourish. This will shape the way we think about life, God, Christianity and the church. Living into new ways of thinking will cultivate a faithful Culture of Imagination among us. Our good friend Christine Sine, who is the Executive Director of Mustard Seed Associates in Seattle, poses this question to us: "Imagine what our lives would be like if we practiced the values of God's kingdom. Imagine what our Christian communities would be like if we lived by the law of love for God and love of neighbor."[11]

My own experience has been one of living into new ways of thinking. I used to think a lot differently about life, God, Christianity and the church. Church was a building or a meeting you went to on Sundays. God was up the sky. Life was about being comfortable and happy. And Christianity was about the forgiveness of sins after you die. But over the course of time, I have come to see things differently. As our fellowship transitioned from being a large, regional service to an on-the-ground practice-based expression in daily life, it changed me. It wasn't just vast

---

[10] Rohr, *Simplicity*, 58.

[11] Sine, *Sacred Rhythms*, 69.

amounts of intellectual learning that changed my thinking, but entering into a practice-based expression, integrated with my studying that shaped me the most.

I remember some of my friends really struggling to understand the importance of shared life in the parish. I think this was primarily because they were not really ready to practice their way into a new way of thinking. They were only searching for understanding with their minds, and consequently they never really experienced an integration. As a result, many of them could not connect and never entered the neighborhood with us. We soon lost contact with many of them as our on-the-ground lives together demanded attention. This has affected me for many years and I still feel a sense of sadness about it, but without practice, revelation is difficult.

I always felt there was something missing in my past experiences of church as a service, or a series of programs, but I didn't really know what to do about it. My friend and mentor Paul Sparks worked with several us to create different experimental environments where we could practice an alternative together. As I participated in learning, reading, listening, and practicing, I slowly became more aware of the importance of things like proximity, locality, shared life, centering in a place, creating a new culture, and embodying life together. I soon moved into the neighborhood reorienting my whole life in the neighborhood of Downtown Tacoma. I have not stopped studying, reading, asking questions, and listening to the wisdom of experienced voices, but I have integrated those with an on-the-ground practice-based theology within the context of our parish. Slowly, the more I practiced my faith, and the more I became present to my place, the more that wisdom began revealing itself to me, however mysteriously. I can no longer think of being part of the church in any other way.

The impossibility and hopelessness we feel toward life could be subverted if the body of Christ were to practice together the things that Jesus taught in a particular place. Our imaginations would come to life and we would be able to dance again. As Brian McLaren says, "practice makes possible some things that would otherwise have been impossible."[12] Everything in life that is wonderful and beautiful takes practice. Will we dare to practice and see the impossible shattered? Will we practice and see the ordinary miracles of everyday life manifested through our relationships?

We need to approach our spirituality in the neighborhood we inhabit with an on-the-ground practice-based theology that is life-giving and filled with hope for all. "Our spirituality needs to become earthy practice that engages with the scruffy and wonderful world of which we are part,"[13] writes Ian Adams. When the body of Christ does not practice together in a place, it will be invisible and nonexistent to those around it. There is no such thing as an invisible body. It is an illusion of our own making.

Stepping into the Way of Sanity: Finding the Courage to be Known

We must have the courage to live relationally and allow ourselves to be known by others. Now of course we will never know each other completely, but as each year passes, if we are present, we can allow ourselves to be known more and more. This is not a fast process; it takes years of sharing life together in a particular place. But without relationship there is no shared life. M. Robert Mulholland Jr. in his book *Invitation to a Journey* stresses a relational spiritual formation in which he says, "Our relationships with others are not only the testing grounds of our spiritual life but also the places where our growth toward wholeness in Christ happens ... But holistic spirituality, the process of being conformed to the image of Christ, takes place in the midst of our relationships with others, not apart from them."[14] We need others to manifest God's goodness and love to us. We also need to be an expression of God's goodness and love to others. The wise monastic Thomas Merton explains:

---

[12] McLaren, *Finding Our Way Again*, 87.

[13] Adams, *Cave Refectory Road*, 24.

[14] Mulholland Jr., *Invitation to a Journey*, 42-43.

Mere living alone does not isolate a man, mere living together does not bring men into communion. The common life can either make one more of a person or less of a person, depending whether it is truly common life or merely life in the crowd. To live in communion, in genuine dialogue with others is absolutely necessary if man is to remain human. But to live in the midst of others, sharing nothing with them but the common noise and the general distraction, isolates a man in the worst way, separates him from reality.[15]

Relational ways of knowing and being known are necessary to our humanity as the body of Christ in local everyday life context. There is so much noise and distraction that keep us from becoming known and relationally whole. How can we rediscover our humanity together in the place that we inhabit? What will bring us into a "genuine dialogue" with one another to know and be known?

Our very capacity to grow in wisdom is dependent upon our relational way of being. Community won't work very well if we do not understand that it is relational. Life is relational. The body of Christ is relational. The Scriptures are relational. The neighborhood is relational. Collaborations and partnerships are relational. People are relational. God is relational. The sacred is relational. The ordinary is relational. In other words, everything in life is relational. All knowing is relational. That is important to understand! Parker J. Palmer writes, "Knowing of any sort is relational, animated by a desire to come into deeper community with what we know."[16]

Sometimes I don't want to be relational. And yet this is the cross that Jesus sets before us as the body of Christ in terms of everyday life together. "If anyone would come after me, he must deny himself and take up his cross and follow me" (Mark 8:34). We follow Jesus by being faithful to our relationships in a particular place. It is hard and difficult

---

[15] Merton, *New Seeds of Contemplation*, p.55.

[16] Palmer, *The Courage to Teach*, 54.

at times, but it is the relational context of the place that we live in that will be the medium that shapes us together into something beautiful.

We always want to allow people to see the good things about us, but not the ugly parts. These we want to hide because they make us look bad. We have to get over this, and just learn to be ourselves with the good and the bad. It is the relational that will slowly heal our depression, loneliness, pain, anger, bitterness and arrogance or whatever else we don't like about ourselves. We seem to be afraid of relational, embodied ways of knowing others and being known. It seems to be too much for us to handle. Our cultural climate often resists the relational. The anti-relational is the matrix from which we all need to be freed.

Shane Claiborne and Jonathan Wilson-Hartgrove remind us that this relational impulse is at the core of our deepest longings. "And so we too are made in the image of community. It's our deepest thirst. We are created to love and to be loved. The biblical story begins and ends with community."[17] We were created in love, intended for love, and exist to be an expression of love. All love is relational. The biblical narrative is intertwined in love. Salvation and redemption is about love. All of Christ's miracles are birthed from love. This relational way of life and love is a community of knowing and being known in a particular place. When we are receptive to God's work in this relational context, it can be the most powerful formative component in shaping us. It is worth quoting Joan Chittister at length:

> In community we work out our connectedness to God, to one another, and to ourselves. It is in community where we find out who we really are. It is life with another that shows my impatience and life with another that demonstrates my possessiveness and life with another that gives notice to my nagging devotion to the self. Life with someone else, in other words, doesn't show me nearly as much about his or her shortcomings as it does about my own. In human relationships I learn how to soften my hard spots and how to reconcile and how to care for someone else besides myself. In

---

[17] Claiborne and Wilson-Hartgrove, *Becoming the Answer to Our Prayers*, 18.

human relationships I learn that theory is no substitute for love. It is easy to talk about the love of God; it is another thing to practice it.[18]

Living relationally within the parish transforms what we think we know about ourselves, about God, and about others. We are pushed to become fully human through relationship. The relationship we have with each person can be a reflection of God to us. God both gives and receives love through relationships with others. The body of Christ cannot be separated from relationship to one another. We need one another to be human. We need one another to learn about our own spirituality.

When we inhabit a neighborhood, that place and the relational connections that we develop there become a part of who we are. They are intertwined with our redemption and salvation. We only know truth through relationship. Without relationship we cannot know anything. Knowing and being known is the truth that will set us free from our own limited imaginations. Knowing and being known relationally will shape who we become as we inhabit the parish throughout the complexities of life. There is no abandoning this relational context when you have experienced it in a place. Christopher L. Heuertz and Christine D. Pohl say in their book *Friendship at the Margins*, "We are who we are because of the communities in which we dwell."[19]

These are the seeds which the Spirit has sown in my own life. These days I can truly say I love my friends in Downtown Tacoma. There are so many special people who have contributed to my life in ways that are hard to communicate. I have been open to live in relationship and have valued those relationships more than anything else in life. Everything else that pulls me away from this relational way of life in the locality of a place is not that important to me anymore. I hope in the years to come I will discover more of what this relational way of knowing and

[18] Chittister, *Wisdom Distilled from the Daily*, 48-49.

[19] Heuertz and Pohl, *Friendship at the Margins*, 126.

being known will reveal about myself, others, God and the body of Christ.

Part 2

A Harsh and Dreadful Love: Embracing the Wisdom of Christ

Chapter 3

Embodying the Way of Love: The Center of Our Life Together

Imitating the Life of Christ: Becoming Local Practitioners

We are all called to imitate the life of Christ in our parish. What does this mean? It means we will love as Christ loved. All of Jesus's life centered around love. He didn't do anything apart from love. The communal imagination needs the life of Jesus living through it. We need to imitate the life of Christ together as the body of Christ in our neighborhood. "Love the Lord your God with all your heart and with all your soul and with all your mind. This is the first and greatest commandment. And the second is like it: Love your neighbor as yourself. All the Law and the Prophets hang on these two commandments" (Matthew 22:37-39). This is what Jesus built his entire human life on. He desired to love others. And by loving others he was loving God the Father. Jesus lived very relationally and loved in the place that he lived. He was a common man among the locals of his time. He was a local practitioner in his context. He walked places and spent time with people.

We imitate Christ whenever we love. That's what he did and he leads his body in the same direction in everyday life. The place we inhabit is the very medium that allows us to be in relationship together so that we can love as Christ exemplified. Christ's love is a mysterious miracle that dances through us in our locality. There is so much need for this love in the relational contexts of everyday life. Imitating Christ's love is divine and miraculous. It is also very ordinary and mundane. We usually cannot understand what is happening when we love. We are drawn to become the church that imitates the life of Christ. The only purpose of the body of Christ today is to become an expression of love. The body needs to learn how to love from the One who is the head of the church in the particulars of everyday life in the parish. What is the body of Christ if there is no love for one another? Simone Weil says, "By loving our neighbor we imitate the divine love which created us."[1]

In my own early experience with my spirituality I had learned doctrines, creeds and lots of theology, but I had not really understood that love within a particular place is so very crucial to allow Christ to live through me. I had become detached from place, detached from relationship, detached from love. All I had were propositional statements and ideas about Christ that weren't manifested as a part of the body of Christ in a particular neighborhood. So I became arrogant and angry. I thought I knew all the answers. And I didn't realize that all knowing is relational and has to do with an embodied expression of love. Without this I can't understand life and God and myself. Over the years I have realized that imitating the life of Christ through love in a particular place is the practice I need in order to discover reality in all of life. I am coming to understand this more, but there is so much more to be discovered. I am living within the question of love. How will my relationships in this place shape me as I love?

"A new commandment I give you: Love one another. As I have loved you, so you must love one another. By this all men will know that you are my disciples, if you love one another" (John 13:34-35). Jesus here is demonstrating how our lives are to be relational and loving. This is what will identify us as his disciples. This is how we imitate Christ. By our

---

[1] Weil, *Waiting for God*, 99.

love we say a lot about what we believe about the gospel. Jesus goes on to say, "If you love me, you will obey what I command" (John 14:15). The obedience he is talking about is our love for others. We need to become a church that is an expression of Christ's love in place, locality and neighborhood. The communal imagination needs to become an expression of love if it is to live.

"I am the light of the world. Whoever follows me will never walk in darkness, but will have the light of life" (John 8:12). Jesus is referring to himself as the light of the world. He is saying that he is the creator and sustainer of all love and light. The light is the love we express and live into. We will walk in love if we imitate Christ. If we follow him, our life will never lead us into the place where there is no love. There are always provisions of love for those who imitate the life of Christ. Love is Christ's nature. Love is his will. Love sustains our existence. Love is a guiding light in our lives together as the body of Christ in the parish. Jesus teaches in the sermon on the mount, "You are the salt of the earth ... You are the light of the world" (Mathew 5:13,14). He is using salt and light as metaphors of the way we are to love in the particular place that we inhabit. Salt preserves. Light guides.

Christ cannot be understood without an embodied life of love on our part. The medium of living within the parish helps us to imitate Christ through love. "If you want to understand Christ's words and relish them fully, you must strive to conform your entire life to His,"[2] writes Thomas a Kempis in his widely read book *The Imitation of Christ*. The conforming piece that we need is the imitation of love. Can we understand anything about Christ without love? I don't really think so. The body of Christ needs to become reconnected to its relationship with love in a particular place. Franciscan Ilia Delio says, "Christ is proclaimed not by words but by the example of one's life ... Christ lives in that Christ lives in us – in our bodies, our hands, our feet and our actions."[3] We are Christ's body to the parish we inhabit in the everyday

---

[2] Kempis, *The Imitation of Christ*, 3.

[3] Delio, *Franciscan Prayer*, 13-14.

particulars of life together. Christ lives through us as his body by our love.

This has been a hard lesson for me to learn. It takes great cultivation of passion and discipline to be a person who is an expression of love in everyday life with others. I have often found myself escaping into hopelessness and confusion within relationships. It is so easy to give up on others and take the cynic's role, saying, "There is no hope or beauty in this relationship. This person is …" Fill in the blank with whatever word or label you would like to place there. There are usually one hundred terms or words I can come up with. This always leads me to depression which is the worst nightmare. My depression does not go away until I start to move toward the communal imagination once again. Often times, it is hard to be depressed when you are seeking to love others with your life. Depression causes me to lose sight of this and turn in on myself while shutting all others out of my thoughts. This is one the worst hells to experience in this life. Christ is leading us out of these hells and into living our lives with the posture of love toward others in the parish.

Our Downtown Neighborhood Fellowship has struggled to love. We have often lost sight of the communal imagination and have resorted to something more like fight club. We have such a hard time thinking about each other and posturing our lives in order to become an expression of love. My friend Liz has grasped a way of love among us. She has modeled for us all what it could look like when we haven't done so well. She makes cards that she gives to others to encourage them, and she prepares dinners where people can be themselves and feel welcomed. Her life is filled with hospitality. She hosts dance parties, wine-tasting get-togethers and times of cooking together with others. She is the retail manager at a local bakery/coffee shop called Corina Bakery which is owned by our friends Mike and Molly. Liz lives a few blocks down the street from the bakery where she can walk or bike to work if she wants. She connects with people all day at the bakery which is a great third place in the neighborhood where people can spend time when they are not at work or home. She is a good listener and has so much compassion, love, grace and kindness toward others. She is constantly loving others in all she does as a way of life in our neighborhood.

Liz teaches me by her love a lot about what it means to believe in the value of others. She has done this for many years and continues by her faithful presence to foster ordinary, relational miracles in everyday life among us as a part of the body of Christ in Downtown Tacoma.

1 Corinthians 13 as a Way of Life: The Most Important Practice of All

My own past experience has been one of trying to explore and discover a capacity to love in the everyday context of life with others with no commitment to a place. This does not work very well. Why is it that I become so angry, irritated, arrogant, fearful, lonely and depressed? My journey has been full of failure and frustration. But when I became involved in the Downtown Neighborhood Fellowship, and we moved into the neighborhood, I began to experience something different. We were exploring our communal imagination to live and love together in a place. It seemed much more holistic. And I soon found peace within myself as I discovered a new perspective on being the body of Christ together in our neighborhood. I was pushed into exploring the capacity to love that lived deep within myself and my friends.

This communal imagination to love in a place will liberate us all to become more human. This has been my own experience. I understand my own humanity better because of the embodied, relational, communal imagination that I am a part of in my neighborhood.

> If I speak in the tongues of men and of angels, but have not love, I am only a resounding gong or a clanging symbol. If I have the gift of prophecy and can fathom all mysteries and all knowledge, and if I have a faith that can move mountains, but have not love, I am nothing. If I give all I possess to the poor and surrender my body to the flames, but have not love, I gain nothing.

Love is patient, love is kind. It does not envy, it does not boast, it is not proud. It is not rude, it is not self-seeking, it is not easily angered, it keeps no record of wrongs. Love does not delight in evil but rejoices with the truth. It always protects, always trusts, always hopes, always perseveres.

Love never fails. But where there are prophecies, they will cease; where there are tongues, they will be stilled; where there is knowledge, it will pass away.

And now these three remain: faith, hope and love. But the greatest of these is love (1 Corinthians 13:1-8,13).

I love this passage of Scripture because it is the major theme of all of the New Testament. Love is the story that we are to enter into. It is everything. We are to inhabit our local context as the body of Christ living into this posture toward all of life. This is what will shape us relationally. I want to become an expression of 1 Corinthians 13 together with my friends in our neighborhood. Thomas Merton states:

When we lose sight of the central element in Christian holiness, which is love, and we forget that the way to fulfill the Christian commandment to love is not something remote and esoteric, but is on the contrary something immediately before us, then the Christian life becomes complicated and very confusing. It loses the simplicity and the unity which Christ gave it in his gospel, and it becomes a labyrinth of unrelated precepts, counsels, ascetic principles, moral cases, and even of legal and ritual technicalities. These things become difficult to understand in proportion as they lose their connection with charity which unites them all and gives them all an orientation to Christ.[4]

Such things as tongues, prophesy, knowledge, giving my body to die in the flames, a faith that can move mountains, giving to the poor, and fathoming mysteries all amount to little without love. I would say that without love everything we do amounts to nothing. Boasting and pride are not a part of love. Being rude and self-seeking is not a part of love.

---

[4] Merton, *Life and Holiness*, 44.

Anger and bitterness is not a part of love. These things are unhealthy for the social capital of our neighborhood. Love is hospitable to patience and kindness. Love is hospitable to celebration and protection. Love is hospitable to trust and hope in others. Love is hospitable toward the strength of perseverance. Faith and hope always stem from love. And love is the greatest quality of our faith as the body of Christ together in the parish.

Without love nothing makes sense in the place that we live. Everything gets really weird really fast without love. How many of us have known people who get really weird by becoming controlling, judgmental, and manipulative around "spiritual" themes or "ministries"? I think this happens because we are not rooting our faith in love. It is rooted in something much more appealing to us. There are a million things to root our faith in besides love and we are being pulled to do just that. But David G. Benner says, "No account of Christian spirituality is complete if it fails to give a central place to love."[5] Love is what makes the communal imagination holistic. Love makes the body of Christ live. Love is what brings healing to our lives. Love builds community in our neighborhood. Love is what will shape the body of Christ in the particulars of everyday life. Love keeps us sane. Love makes us human in so many ways.

John M. Perkins, founder of the Christian Community Development Association, emphasizes that, "Loving each other ... might just be the greatest thing we can do."[6] Our love could be the thing that brings liberation to us all in the parish. Our love is to be a part of our salvation, redemption and sanctification as the body of Christ. As we live together in the proximity of a neighborhood, we will all be shaped through relationship. We can become great through love. We cannot become great in any other way! Our love as the body of Christ together in the particulars of everyday life will do miracles among us.

---

[5] Benner, *Sacred Companions*, 32.

[6] Claiborne and Perkins, *Follow Me to Freedom*, 168.

How we show that we are spiritually attuned to reality is by our love. Love is the way of a relational life in the parish. Love guides and teaches us how to discern what is real. Love is the only relevant factor in our relationships within the body of Christ in the particulars of everyday life. "There is one thing we must understand, however," writes William A. Meninger, "and that is that our love must dominate our action and give it direction."[7] If love is not present within us, we literally have nothing to build our faith on together. If love dies within us, we soon become less than human. We become objects to the systems of our culture and cease to be a "peculiar people" in our local context. Love must possess and dominate all that we do. Love must shape us and change us constantly. Love must capture our imaginations and become communal in the place where we live. Everything we do must stem from this love that Paul is talking about in 1 Corinthians 13.

We need to see our lives as the expression of this 1 Corinthians 13 love as the body of Christ in the particulars of everyday life together in the parish. This is God's will for us. We cannot escape the call. Our local context will teach us how to love, being kind to one another and showing patience. This begins in the particulars of life now. The relational context we find ourselves in will constantly manifest love all around us. Catherine Doherty says, "The kingdom of God, which is the kingdom of love, begins here and now."[8]

God is already working in the neighborhood all around us in our locality if we would only become aware of what is going on. The neighborhood is the medium where we learn to love relationally. The communal imagination will be cultivated through this 1 Corinthians 13 way of life in the particulars of each situation we find ourselves in. Love is calling out to us relationally in all of life. Every relationship brings opportunities to love. This is what should define us over the course of our lives.

---

[7] Meninger, *The Loving Search for God*, 25.

[8] Doherty, *Poustinia*, 155.

Love has been a hard reality for me to face as I have tried to reduce following Christ to something else. My local context always calls me back to the reality of relational love toward others when I tend to do this. God is constantly teaching me through the relational context of the neighborhood that love is all that matters. Anything less will not do. So many times I have lost the focus of this 1 Corinthians 13 love. But I am coming to understand that this is what I need to base my life on. Jesus is calling to me through the seasons of life, through the wind I feel on my face as I walk outside in my neighborhood, to love. I cannot ignore this call to love. I cannot ignore this call to the parish. I cannot ignore this call to live relationally.

So much of my life has been an evasion of love in the parish. I am beginning to understand that God is calling me to love others with real faces in front of me. I don't like the responsibility of this. It is too much. It is too harsh and dreadful. I shout out in the night, "Leave me alone to myself!" I don't want to give my life for others in this way. Love has no relevance to me at times like this. Sometimes I am a failure in learning to love, but my failure is also my teacher. I am learning to love those who are my neighbors and finding the commonalities between us. The parish is teaching me to love. The parish is shaping me.

The Downtown Neighborhood Fellowship has struggled to learn to love over the years in the place we find ourselves in. We have struggled to love others. But our struggle is revealing to us more and more how to love relationally. We are on our way to becoming a faithful presence of love to our neighborhood. God is working out our salvation relationally in the particulars of everyday life together. We have suffered sometimes and have seen many people come and go in our lives. There have been good times and bad times. But through it all we desire to love even if we can't tell what it will amount to or if it will amount to anything at all. When we love, we sometimes feel like we have lost. We give so much of our lives and we receive what seems to be so little in return. But we have to remind ourselves it is always worth loving others no matter what we understand about it.

Seeing Value and Mystery in and Through Others: Transforming Our Perceptions

I like the part of the creation story where God creates human beings in his own image. "Then God said, 'Let us make man in our image, in our likeness.' So God created man in his own image, in the image of God he created him; male and female he created them" (Genesis 1:26,27). This is so mysterious and beautiful, that our God could create humanity in his goodness and creativity. What a marvelous thought! I am made in the image of God and so are my friends in the neighborhood.

Every person is so valuable to our Creator. James M. Houston notes, "If God created us in his own image, to be like him, then every single person has an incalculable value."[9] Every person in their humanity is created with such deep value and mystery. It is so valuable that when this value and mystery lies undiscovered, we live with a disability in our self-perceptions that scar us our whole lives.

We hold such value and mystery toward one another in the parish. Everyday relational life should be focused on drawing out these assets. Doing so cultivates the communal imagination. Searching for the value and mystery in others is one of the ways we learn to love. It is there, we just have to find it. Barbara Brown Taylor articulates this well, "The point is to see the person standing right in front of me, who has no substitute, who can never be replaced, whose heart holds things for which there is no language, whose life is an unsolved mystery. The moment I turn that person into a character in my own story, the encounter is over. I have stopped being a human being and have become a fiction writer instead."[10]

I cannot turn others into an object to be manipulated. I must see their mystery. I must see their value. Anything less makes me less than human. We need to encourage our mutual humanity by learning to see

---

[9] Houston, *The Prayer*, 23.

[10] Taylor, *An Altar in the World*, 102.

the value and mystery within each of us because we are all created in the image of God. The body of Christ in the parish has to nurture this value and mystery in others. This is where the relational miracles will take place among us, when our value and mystery are liberated.

This is the way Christ related to the people of his day.

> Now one of the Pharisees invited Jesus to have dinner with him, so he went to the Pharisee's house and reclined at the table. When a women who had lived a sinful life in that town learned that Jesus was eating at the Pharisees house, she brought an alabaster jar of perfume, and as she stood behind him at his feet weeping, she began to wet his feet with her tears. Then she wiped them with her hair, kissed them and poured perfume on them.
>
> When the Pharisee who had invited him saw this, he said to himself, "If this man were a prophet, he would know who is touching him and what kind of woman she is—that she is a sinner."
>
> Jesus answered him, "Simon, I have something to tell you."
>
> "Tell me, teacher," he said.
>
> "Two men owed money to a certain moneylender. One owed him five hundred denarii, and the other fifty. Neither of them had the money to pay him back, so he canceled the debts of both. Now which of them will love him more?"
>
> Simon replied, "I suppose the one who had the bigger debt canceled."
>
> "You have judged correctly," Jesus said.
>
> Then he turned toward the woman and said to Simon, "Do you see this woman? I came into your house. You did not give me any water for my feet, but she wet my feet with her tears and wiped them with her hair. You did not give me a kiss, but this woman, from the time I entered, has not stopped kissing my feet. Therefore, I tell you, her many sins have been forgiven—for she

loved much. But he who has been forgiven little loves little" (Luke 7:36-47).

I like this story because Jesus is seeing the value and mystery in this woman whom others saw as something less than beautiful. Others saw her as "sinful" and wrote her off as having nothing of value or mystery. She was just who they thought her to be. But Jesus saw her for who she was, as a person created in the image of God. She had value and mystery to Jesus. She had human worth to Jesus. He probably had known this woman in his local context and saw how others had constantly made her to be something less than human. Jesus wanted to show everyone what the kingdom of God is like relationally through his interaction with this woman. Others had a hard time grasping the love that Christ was demonstrating toward this woman. And yet this is how we are called to love: by seeing the value and mystery in others in the place where we live.

Why is it so hard to see this value and mystery in and through others? It seems that our lives have been blinded to this relational capacity of love in the parish. But the communal imagination will settle for nothing less. The communal imagination needs to see through the paradigm of value and mystery when embodying a relational way of life locally. This is the subversion we need in order to be the body of Christ together in the particulars of everyday life. Gus Gordon explains, "Every person is a visible image of the invisible Mystery and therefore has an inalienable dignity and absolute significance that is not dependent on nationality, race, sex, or economic status or on any human moral condition, human labor, or accomplishment."[11]

Being a North American white guy has been difficult for me sometimes because the larger culture of the United States usually does not value as highly those of other races and countries. Being elevated over others because my race and country is not something I like very much. I have been on a path of questioning all of this. Why are some races and

---

[11] Gordon, *Solitude and Compassion*, 108.

countries valued more than others? It all seems strange to me. Just because North America possesses the most power and wealth on earth does not make it special. Learning to subvert this mindset in order to practice seeing the value and mystery in others regardless of race or country has recently been shaping me in the parish.

My friend Larry is a Native American man who is homeless. He grew up in a dysfunctional home. His father was not there for him. Larry often stole stuff from stores because he did not have much growing up. He soon found himself in juvenile detention and he dropped out of high school. Larry was shipped around to foster homes where he did not receive much care. He now is in his fifties and has lived on the streets for a long time.

One day when I was walking home after a movie, I saw him sleeping in the bushes off of Fawcett Street. He regularly comes to the Catholic Worker House in our neighborhood to take a shower and socialize on the porch with others. His life seems sad to most people who live in houses and apartments, but I am discovering how God cares for Larry just as much as he cares for me. I am coming out of my blindness to see Larry in all his mystery and value as a human being. It is fascinating how much I learn from Larry as I spend time with him. He loves the sitcom *Friends* from the 90's. I believe it resonates with him because he longs for friends and human connection like all of us. Larry does not like to be lonely, but oftentimes that is his experience. He is always so cheerful, respectful and kind. He is a model to me of the caring presence of Jesus in our midst. I don't know if Larry thinks of himself this way, but Christ lives in and through the poor among us.

Keshane is another friend in whom I have learned to see his mystery and value over the years. He is an African-American in his late thirties. At over six feet tall, he is a big, intimidating-looking man. Most people would probably be afraid of him if they saw him on the streets late at night. Keshane has that kind of a presence, but as I have gotten to know him a little, he is very much a gentle person in whom I see the image of God.

For many years, Keshane has struggled with addiction. He went to prison for five years for arson, theft and drug possession. He never wants to go back to prison. It was hard for him and he has shared with me frightening stories of life behind bars. Keshane likes to work out in the park doing push-ups, pull-ups and sit–ups, and running. I see him sometimes on the streets in our neighborhood hanging around after getting a milkshake or whatever.

I am learning to really live through the example of Keshane and his passion to stay alive. He does not want to die as have so many of his friends. He wants to live a better life. He wants a future. And those are some of the same things that I too want. Keshane is showing me what life is and how to cultivate a passion for the things I care about in life. The mystery and value I see in Keshane is teaching me to keep dreaming without getting discouraged.

I love my friend Alfredo. He is an immigrant from Mexico. He lives in the same house as me and doesn't really like to speak English that much. In his seventies, Alfredo's health is getting worse as he ages. He is having problems with his eyes and has a hard time walking a lot of the time. Watching action movies is one of his favorite things to do along with listening to Spanish music in the mornings with some good coffee. Alfredo is dear to me because he relies on others for his life. He has lived at the Guadalupe House Tacoma Catholic Worker in our neighborhood for nearly twenty two years and has been deported from the United States many times. Alfredo has no family, but the Catholic Worker has been his home.

I like Alfredo because he is teaching me to not get caught up in the narrative of upward mobility but to just rest in my friendships where I live. This is so countercultural and almost nonexistent in our times in North America. Alfredo is teaching me to not talk so much. I am learning to listen instead and just be in someone's presence. This is one of the most mysterious relational practices that I have learned over the years in the parish. He is constantly teaching me of his unique value and mystery in everyday life as I learn to see Christ in him.

Loving others by seeing the value and mystery in and through them is about having the imagination to see Christ in others. This is a radical thought! Does Christ really live in each and every one of us even if we have not "accepted Christ" into our lives? I think he does in some mysterious way that we cannot always understand. I believe there are dimensions of Christ that live in all of us. How could they not? We are created in his image. Not some people but all people. Dorothy Day encourages us "To love with understanding and without understanding. To love blindly, and to folly. To see only what is lovable. To think only on these things. To see the best in everyone around, their virtues rather than their faults. To see Christ in them."[12] This is what the body of Christ is called to in the parish.

Respecting the image of God which lives inside us all will bring some sanity to our broken relationships. We will begin to heal and bring life to others when this happens. Seeing the value and mystery in others keeps us from labeling and boxing them up and instead be who they are in their humanity. We refuse to cut off someone from the value and mystery that God has given them. If I cannot see the value and mystery in you, you become nothing to me. The communal imagination always sees the value and mystery in others. Thomas Keating writes, "To love one's neighbor as oneself is to respect the image of God in our neighbor with all the rights of which that dignity confers. To love one another as Jesus loves us is to love one another in our humanness—in our individuality and opinionatedness, in personality conflicts and in unbearable situations. It is to continue to show love, no matter what the provocation may be to act otherwise."[13]

---

[12] Day, *On Pilgrimage*, 255.

[13] Keating, *Invitation to Love*, 109.

Chapter 4

Listening to Our Faithful Presence: Being Shaped by the Parish

Being Faithfully Present: Experiencing the Gospel through One Another

My friends Melody, Liz, Nora, Dotti, Theresa, Cathy and Karen are a part of a collaboration of women in the neighborhood called the Madrinas, meaning "the godmothers." They strive to be godmothers to the neighborhood providing relational care in everyday life. This association began out of a deeper integration between our Downtown Neighborhood Fellowship and the Tacoma Catholic Worker. All of the women involved have been rooted in the neighborhood for a while now.

Striving to work for the common good of the parish is what they care about. They create spaces for nurturing common interests and developing friendships. The Madrinas are always seeking out ways to be faithfully present and available to others. They are being shaped by their many of years of living, working and collaborating in the neighborhood. Honoring the lives of others is something they value. Being shaped interdependently and working together collectively is a way of life for them. It seems they are always dialoging about hospitality to the poor and how they can be a faithful presence against gentrification in our downtown development. They seek to find their voice in a society dominated by patriarchy and violence.

The Madrinas are organizing a renovation plan of the backyard area of the Guadalupe house in our neighborhood which has a big yard with a lot of space including a community garden. They are working on developing a meditation garden on the south side of the house, leveling the backyard, creating a community gathering place, redesigning the garden so it is easier to maintain, and creating a playground for children. They have had a bunch of meetings where neighbors can come together to collaborate and dream of what they want to see happen. The collaboration ranges from local business owners, to gardeners, to the poor, to artists, to all kinds of neighbors younger and older, male and female. We are all excited to see what will happen in the years to come through this initiative. It is a demonstration of how to create environments through our relationships where we can experience the gospel through one another. The love that the neighborhood experiences through the Madrinas is an embodiment of relational care by expressing beauty in the neighborhood.

"For where two or three come together in my name, there I am with them" (Mathew 18:20). I see this passage relating to our presence to one to another. When we are together in the particulars of everyday life, Christ is holding us together with and through his love. When we are present to one another in the local context of our neighborhood, there is a great amount of love that is being given and received. We need to come together in the particulars of life as the body of Christ with a posture of faithful presence to one another.

This is an appropriate expression of love. The communal imagination is one of relational presence to others. When we are physically together with others, but not emotionally present, this is not relational. It doesn't foster love. It is treating people as less than human. What a tragedy that in so many of our relationships we are not truly present to one another. God wants the body of Christ to be faithfully present to one another in the parish. If the body of Christ cannot be present it cannot love. And this presence to our parish is what will shape us as we live, work and play there. David G. Benner says:

> Presence begins with attentiveness. This demands that I focus on the other person ... This attentiveness to the other involves setting some things aside. It usually means setting aside my own interests and preoccupations. It also demands that I stop analyzing what I am hearing or rehearsing how I will respond. And ... it also involves resisting the impulse to solve problems or fix things that appear broken.[1]

We need to stop trying to change or fix others. This is the call of being present to others out of love for them. Presence has an attentiveness to it. We need to be present to one another as friends who care deeply and love. We will have to let go of some control. We will have to let go of the cliché that we can "change the world." This vision is too big, too abstract. Let's get down to what is right in front of us: real people in real life contexts who live in our neighborhood. These are the people we are called to love and become faithfully present to relationally.

Faithful presence takes time. It is slow. It is organic. It is not a project or program. It is real face-to-face relationship in the context of everyday life together. This is such a challenge and this relational presence will test our faith as the body of Christ.

> At that time the kingdom of heaven will be like ten virgins who took their lamps and went out to meet the bridegroom. Five of them were foolish and five were wise. The foolish ones took their lamps but did not take any oil with them. The wise, however, took oil in jars along with their lamps. The bridegroom was a long time in coming, and they all became drowsy and fell asleep.
>
> At midnight the cry rang out: "Here's the bridegroom! Come out to meet him!"

---

[1] Benner, *Sacred Companions*, 50.

Then all the virgins woke up and trimmed their lamps. The foolish ones said to the wise, "Give us some of your oil; our lamps our going out."

"No," they replied, "there may not be enough for both us and you. Instead, go to those who sell oil and buy some for yourselves."

But while they were on their way to buy oil, the bridegroom arrived. The virgins who were ready went in with him to the wedding banquet. And the door was shut.

Later the others also came. "Sir!" "Sir!" they said. "Open the door for us!"

But he replied, "I tell you the truth, I don't know you."

Therefore keep watch, because you do not know the day or the hour" (Matthew 25:1-13).

I find this parable fascinating. Maybe it has a lot to do with being present to others as a way of being present to Christ in our local context. The five wise virgins were present and ready when the bridegroom came to get them because they had the right amount of oil for their lamps so that they could see. The five foolish virgins were not present to the bridegroom. They did not make sure they had enough oil for their lamps. The body of Christ is the bride of Christ, and Christ is the bridegroom. How Christ reveals himself as the bridegroom is through others in relationship in the context of everyday life. We need to be like the five wise virgins who were ready and prepared when the bridegroom arrived. The bridegroom always manifests himself through our love, our presence to one another in relationship. Through being present relationally to others in the parish, we become ready to encounter the bridegroom through all kinds of relational encounters.

We never know what will happen as we are faithfully present. We just might experience all kinds of miraculous wedding banquet-like celebrations through relationship, revealing wisdom and love as we follow the example of the five wise virgins. Jesus is teaching that the way to be present to him is to be present to others out of love. We will miss out on all kind of wisdom and relational revelations in the parish if we are not present to others. Richard Rohr states in one of my favorite books *The Naked Now*:

> Wisdom is not the gathering of more facts and information, as if that would eventually coalesce into truth. Wisdom is precisely a different way of seeing and knowing those ten thousand things. I suggest that wisdom is precisely the freedom to be present. Wise people always know how to be present, but it is much more then that. Presence is wisdom! People who are fully present know how to see fully, rightfully, and truthfully. Presence is the one thing necessary, and in many ways, the hardest thing of all. Just try to keep your heart open, your mind without division or resistance, and your body not somewhere else. Presence is the practical, daily task of all mature religion and all spiritual disciplines.[2]

Rohr says elsewhere, "Let me describe the effect of presence in this way. The mystery of presence is that encounter wherein the self-disclosure of one evokes a deeper life in the other. There is nothing you need to 'think' or understand to be present; it is all about giving and receiving right now, and it is not done in the mind. It is actually a transference and sharing of Being."[3]

Presence has been a hard lesson for me to learn even though I have lived in the same place, locality and neighborhood for a number of years now. The love that is demanded in order to be faithfully present to others in everyday life can be harsh and dreadful. It requires a sharing of my very being with someone. But this is how we love. And this is how we are shaped. This is how we experience the gospel in everyday life. We cannot love without being present. "True presence," states Gunilla Norris, "requires that we be attentive to what is happening here and now. It is an offering of our awareness, our participation, and our

---

[2] Rohr, *The Naked Now*, 59-60.

[3] Rohr, *Things Hidden*, 64.

willingness."[4] We need the body of Christ to be present to others in the particulars of everyday life in the parish.

Listening to Others: Being Slow to Make a Sound

There is so much talking today within the body of Christ. There is an overemphasis on preaching and converting others through words and information. When will we ever learn how to listen instead of preaching so much? Listening is much harder than talking all the time. What would happen if we had an experimental approach to listening in the particulars of everyday life together in the parish? I think we would see amazing things happen. Love is intertwined with listening. Without listening, does love even exist within us? The communal imagination has a desire for listening. Listening is the foundation of all relational love in the parish.

I remember when our Downtown Neighborhood Fellowship first moved into the neighborhood to become a local expression of the body of Christ. We had to learn how to listen to each other and those in the neighborhood. If we didn't love, we could not get along very well. We had to grow in our love for others through a new paradigm of listening.

Our way of witnessing was to listen. We started to build trust with one another and with others in the neighborhood who were skeptical about Christianity through listening. Now after years of listening, we have come to be better friends with our neighbors in the parish. All kinds of things have developed out of us expressing our love for others just by listening. We would have been driven out by the locals if we didn't learn how to listen and respect them. Listening can drastically change the body of Christ as we share the particulars of everyday life in the parish.

Our Downtown Neighborhood Fellowship has done a lot of training and practice around listening. We have created intentional practices with one another to hear our particular stories through one person

---

[4] Norris, *Inviting Silence*, 53.

asking questions, and another person recording the story without saying a word to the other person. In this process there is no giving advice or commenting, it is just pure listening. We have found how transforming this can be when we approach it with our whole being. We are becoming shaped by the stories of another who is different from us, but who also has similarities. We have found solidarity with one another in our neighborhood because of our intentional practices of listening. We listen to one another, our neighbors, our parish and our God.

I had never heard of such a thing as the spirituality of listening before I had met my friend Paul. In my life before moving into the neighborhood, all I knew was a spirituality of communicating through words. This fascinated me because I saw how the church was not connecting very well with the North American culture, especially where I lived in the Northwest. Knowing something was not right for many years and becoming frustrated, God soon led me to this spirituality of embodiment and listening in the parish. This has resonated so deeply within me that I will live this out the rest of my life. How amazing it would be to live in my particular neighborhood for the next fifty years! I could become a faithful presence of goodness, love and beauty working in collaboration within Downtown Tacoma with so many friends and neighbors. That would be a grace of God and an ordinary miracle if God provided me the strength to be that kind of leader in my parish.

After we moved into the neighborhood, we met some great people who were clearly caring for this place long before we were here. Two were our friends Trish and Thane. They were such an example to us because they actually lived, worked and played in the neighborhood of Downtown Tacoma. They owned a big building in the neighborhood and also ran two businesses. One was a hair salon and the other was a smoothie and juice bar. Thane remodeled the building so that they could live there and run the businesses from their new home. We all thought that this was so inspiring! We had neighbors who were caring for this place along with us and were much more connected relationally than we were. Trish started a campaign in our neighborhood called Go

Local in which she encourages others to live and shop locally rather than go outside of the neighborhood. These are things we had learned a lot about from Trish and Thane as we became friends, neighbors and collaborators on behalf of the neighborhood.

We have invested much in listening to our good friends in this way. Trish and Thane do not necessarily see themselves as following the example of Christ, but to us they are examples of the relational care that the gospel calls us all to. Our Downtown Neighborhood Fellowship is extremely grateful for neighbors like Trish and Thane, whom we took the time to notice and listen to. We have discovered that God works in all kinds of ways if we will just listen deeply.

Christ was a listener. He loved people. He lived relationally in his local context. How could he not be? Jesus' baptism by John the Baptist was a profound act of listening on Jesus's part.

> Then Jesus came from Galilee to the Jordan to be baptized by John. But John tried to deter him, saying, "I need to be baptized by you, and do you come to me?"
>
> Jesus replied, "Let it be so now, it is proper for us to do this to fulfill all righteousness." Then John consented (Matthew 3:13-15).

John thought that he should be the one receiving from Jesus, but Jesus didn't agree. Instead, he wanted to listen to John and submit to him. How backwards is that? Maybe Jesus is giving us an example to follow about how to learn to submit to others and to listen more than talk or push our agenda. It was in listening to and being directed by John that all righteousness was fulfilled.

Jesus would have it no other way. Just think about the death of Christ. It also was a profound act of listening to his Father, and in the context of listening to others (all the prophets who went before him). You might think that Jesus preached and taught a lot in the Scriptures. But that was only during a few years of his life. Before that, he had lived about thirty years in his local context where he learned to listen and love. What if we lived somewhere for thirty years, learning to love and listen, before we started teaching about the gospel?

Listening builds trust. Listening brings healing to relationships. Listening lets go of controlling life. Listening cultivates the communal imagination in the parish. The struggle of listening is worth it all. We gain so much relational wisdom through listening to others. Relational revelations are drenched in listening. We can love others by having a listening posture in all of life. "To listen deeply can be a struggle because we have to let go of our agenda," says Jan Johnson, "and the need to defend ourselves or the desire to persuade people to see things our way."[5]

We all need listening more than we realize as an expression of love to bring us together in the particulars of everyday life. All relational contexts flourish through listening. Listening will do ordinary miracles among us as the years play out in our lives together in the parish. How can we be closed off to listening? A life without a listening posture is a life that is lost. Keri Wyatt Kent says, "Listening is a gift that can bring us together."[6] She goes on to say, "Listening communicates love."[7]

Without listening we become arrogant toward and disrespectful of others. We destroy our relationships and bring on the unconscious suicide of our personality. We slowly deteriorate and do not carry ourselves well. We become blind and ignorant. We become self-centered and begin to hate. As a matter of fact, all hate stems from a refusal to listen. We are not called to hate as the body of Christ, but we are called to love. And love is about listening in the parish. "To live without listening is not to live at all; it is simply to drift in my own backwater,"[8] writes the wise Benedictine Joan Chittister. In other

---

[5] Johnson, *Invitation to the Jesus Life*, 50.

[6] Kent, *Listen*, 106

[7] Ibid., 91.

[8] Chittister, *Wisdom Distilled from the Daily*, 21.

words, when we don't listen, we die. We are living a slow agonizing death without listening. God is a listener and we are made in his image to listen.

"My dear brothers, take note of this: Everyone should be quick to listen." (James 1:19). James is encouraging us to listen. He urges us to "take note of this." That means he thinks it is important. I think there is a lot of correlation here with Paul's encouragement in 1 Corinthians 13 to love above all things. Listening as a way to express our love for others is so important to the body of Christ in place, locality and neighborhood. The particulars of everyday life need a fabric of relationships where listening is active and alive. Again Keri Wyatt Kent says, "Our listening communicates love, often more clearly than our words."[9] The communal imagination needs to listen if it is to communicate love. There is no way around this. Listening precedes a lot of other less important things that might seem more "spiritual" to us. In fact, listening is deeply spiritual and deeply relational.

Thich Nhat Hanh observes such truth when he writes, "Deep listening is the basis for reconciliation."[10] Could this possibly be so? If listening really leads to reconciliation, then the members of the body of Christ have found the key to getting along with each other and those they live with in the neighborhood in the particulars of everyday life. This would be truly miraculous. As I said before, it is in the ordinary, relational particulars of everyday life that God manifests his miracles. Listening as a means to reconciliation has a big part to play in this. This doesn't seem "spiritual" to us, but it is: Listening is infused with the miraculous, particular, ordinary aspects of relational living in the parish. What good news to our lives! Listening is life- giving, and we can all do it through the guidance of Christ, who is the head of the body.

---

[9] *Listen*, 73.

[10] Nhat Hanh, *Touching Peace*, 88.

Intentionality: Cultivating Relational Connection

There needs to be intentionality to our love as the body of Christ in the particulars of everyday life in the parish. Without some intentionality we will not become an expression of Christ's love in our neighborhood. "Therefore, my dear friends, as you have always obeyed—not only in my presence, but now much more in my absence—continue to work out your salvation with fear and trembling, for it is God who works in you to will and act according to his good purpose" (Philippians 2:12-13).

We need to work out our salvation as the body of Christ together through our love with intentionality and seriousness. If there is no intentionality, there will be little love to share in our lives. Our intentionality will guide our love for others in the parish. We need some discernment around what this will contextually means for us. God's will for us is to love and to work out our salvation together. Being intentional about our presence, listening and seeing the value and mystery in others is a starting point to this intentional way of love. Without intentionality, we struggle to be relational in all of life. Without intentionality, we conform to the culture around us and thus lose the peculiar call on our lives. We become like a lot of people who live in our culture with little meaning and a lot of hopelessness. Working out our salvation disciplines us in giving our lives to become an expression of love in the particulars of everyday life together.

My friend Nichole has been a natural connector in our neighborhood for a number of years now. She has chosen to live intentionally in Downtown Tacoma by becoming an expression of love to all kinds of neighbors in everyday life. Nichole has embraced the limitations of place, but has also embraced the synergy this creates by connecting with those often around her. She is no longer secluded from others, but is open and hospitable to her neighbors in sharing her life with them.

When Nichole first moved to our neighborhood, she intentionally chose six or seven places that were locally owned to spend time in. She was constantly asking, "What does love look like here?" and "What is my responsibility?" Themes of love, reconciliation and growth were constantly on her mind. She started to really listen to what the place and the people were saying to her.

This led Nichole to start an intentional exploration around gratitude, ego, and presence which helped her to love more freely in everyday life. Nichole started to notice the small details of the ordinary moments of life and how they matter a lot in caring for others. She wanted to start showing up emotionally when she was with others instead of just withdrawing emotionally even while she was physically present. She noticed how she was being driven by power and fear. This made it difficult to enter into a way of life that supported her being.

What became apparent to her as she interacted with others was she sensed herself being driven either by her ego or the love within her. In response, Nichole learned to practice a faithful presence to others which took a lot of courage, vulnerability and awareness. She became heard and seen in our neighborhood in a way that frightened her at first, but which has also led to healing and peace. Now after many years of intentionally loving others, she is one of the most connected people in Downtown Tacoma. Nichole is known as a woman of love, peace and joy to our neighbors. Her life is the fruit of Christ living in her through gentleness, sensitivity, and grace.

"But whatever was to my profit I now consider loss for the sake of Christ. What is more, I consider everything a loss compared to the surpassing greatness of knowing Christ Jesus my Lord, for whose sake I have lost all things. I consider them rubbish, that I may gain Christ and may be found in him not, having a righteousness of my own that comes from the law, but that which is through faith in Christ—the righteousness that comes from God and is by faith. I want to know Christ and the power of his resurrection and the fellowship of sharing in his sufferings, becoming like him in his death, and so, somehow, to attain to his resurrection from the dead" (Philippians 3:7-11).

Paul is saying here how he wants to pursue knowing Christ so single-
mindedly that he will intentionally forsake everything else in order to
do this. Nothing else matters to him. What does all this mean? How
can we have some discernment around these themes? To pursue
knowing Christ with this high degree of intentionality is what we are
being called into. We are constantly coming to know Christ more as we
love others intentionally.

This intentionality is to be lived out within the context of the parish
through our love. As we love, we begin to understand Christ more and
more. There is the power of Christ's resurrection within us, a sharing in
the fellowship of his sufferings, and we become more like him through
the process of love. Having an intentional love for others sets this all in
motion. It is the working out of our salvation. Ruth Haley Barton
states:

> We generally think of indifference as a negative attitude that is
> characterized by apathy and not caring; in the realm of
> discernment, however, indifference is a very positive term that is
> rich in meaning. Here it means "I am indifferent to anything but
> God's will." This is a state of wide openness to God in which I am
> free from undue attachment to any particular outcome, and I am
> capable of relinquishing whatever might keep me from choosing
> for love. I have gotten to a place where I want God and his will
> more than anything—more than ego gratification, more than
> looking good in the eyes of others, more than personal ownership
> or comfort or advantage. I want "God's will, nothing more, nothing
> less, nothing else." For any of us human beings to come to this
> place of indifference is no small thing."[11]

Indifference to everything else in our life has a lot to do with
intentionality in regards to love. Just as Paul considered everything
rubbish compared to his pursuit of knowing Christ, we too should be
indifferent to everything except to know Christ through loving others
in the parish. What if our love for others was more important to us
than our personal comfort, our ego agendas, our reputation, our

---

[11] Barton, *Sacred Rhythms*, 119.

economic status, our career or our family? What a radical thought! This should not be so strange to us, but I think it is. God longs for his body to demonstrate and express love together in the particulars of everyday life. Our intentionality to love and our indifference to everything that keeps us from God's will for us to love one another is the posture that will help us to work out our salvation together.

Dorothy Day, the legendary Catholic social activist, says, "It is an easy thing to talk about love, but it is something to be proven, to be suffered, to be learned."[12] To be intentional about love is all good in theory to many of us, but in practice it is not so desirable. Love has to be learned through much practice. We are not so good at it as the body of Christ. We have to be intentional, willing to go through the suffering that love will bring our way. We have to prove our love through building trust and sacrificing for others. That is why listening is so important to an intentional love in and for the parish. Intentionality will call us to a harsh and dreadful love for others. There is no running from this kind of intentionality if we want to live in the real world.

The intentionality that love demands is very straightforward and will not be reduced to keeping rules and not doing bad things. We are called to so much more in the particulars of everyday life as the body of Christ. Looking for the opportunities all around us in the parish to love intentionally is what gives life to the body of Christ. The communal imagination needs this intentionality of love to live and work out its salvation. "Love is other-centered and action-orientated," Bruxy Cavey writes. "According to Jesus, it isn't good enough NOT to do bad, we must look for opportunities to actively do good! We must look for opportunities to express the practical care and loving concern to others that we would want expressed to us."[13] Isn't this the intentionality we must have to love in the parish? Are we looking for opportunities to love relationally as the body of Christ?

---

[12] Day, *On Pilgrimage*, 125.

[13] Cavey, *The End of Religion*, 188.

How can it be any other way? Remember, without an intentionality to love everything comes to nothing. The whole purpose of our spirituality and connection to the body of Christ is to love intentionally. There is no other option for us than to be intentional about loving others in the place that we live. We need to be serious about working out our salvation in this way. Hugh Feiss writes, "People who love as the Gospels require aim to be alive."[14] We seek to live when we love with intentionality. We seek God when we love with intentionality. The communal imagination is intertwined with this intentionality to love as the body of Christ in the parish.

Love must be nurtured by intentionality and practice in the parish. Love will not live within us without an intentional practice of being in relationship with others. Those who seem different from us will teach us to love. Diversity and uniqueness keep the gospel alive among us. God has created everyone uniquely; no two people are exactly alike. We need to cultivate and nurture this intentional love by learning to acknowledge our common humanity and live in solidarity with others. We may be different on some levels, but we all have a lot in common if we have the imagination to discover this. The communal imagination likes diversity and uniqueness. The value and mystery of others is drawn out in diversity and uniqueness. Our intentionality will hold our love in God's hands to multiply and increase within the body of Christ in the place we inhabit. Every bit of our being is to be given to this intentionality to love so that relational miracles can happen in our local context.

Macrina Wiederkehr says: "In your contacts with people each day, you will be blessed if you remember that your work is your love poured out."[15] Wiederkehr is not talking about the "blessing" of American wealth, status and prestige. She is talking about the blessings of living out the kingdom of God within us.

---

14 Feiss, *Essential Monastic Wisdom*, 182.

15 Wiederkehr, *Seven Sacred Pauses*, 73.

Blessed are the poor in spirit, for theirs is the kingdom of God. Blessed are those who mourn, for they will be comforted. Blessed are the meek, for they will inherit the earth. Blessed are those who hunger and thirst for righteousness, for they will be filled. Blessed are the merciful, for they will be shown mercy. Blessed are the pure in heart, for they will see God. Blessed are the peacemakers, for they will be called sons of God. Blessed are those who are persecuted because of righteousness, for theirs is the kingdom of heaven. Blessed are you when people insult you, persecute you and falsely say all kinds of evil against you because of me. Rejoice and be glad, because great is your reward in heaven, for in the same way they persecuted the prophets who were before you (Matthew 5:3-12).

This all stems from an intentional relational way of love in the parish. When we give our lives intentionally to become expressions of Christ's love together we will be blessed by the relational revelations that are given to us. The body of Christ needs these to survive the changing times of our culture. When our love is freely given to others without ceasing in the particulars of everyday life, we will be the body of Christ together- and together working out our salvation.

Chapter 5

Celebrating the Small Things: The Foundation of Living Relationally

Doing the Small Things: Valuing What Seems Not to Matter

It is in the small things where love is most alive among us. It seems Christ valued the small things in life that nobody else saw. He always loved in a seemingly small way through the particulars of everyday life. Others saw Jesus as small and no big deal. But Christ always works through the small, ordinary, particulars of everyday common life.

> Jesus sat down opposite the place where the offerings were put and watched the crowd putting their money into the temple treasury. Many rich people threw in large amounts. But a poor widow came and put in two very small copper coins, worth only a fraction of a penny.
>
> Calling his disciples to him, Jesus said, "I tell you the truth, this poor widow has put more into the treasury than all the others. They all gave out of their wealth; but she, out of her poverty, put in everything—all she had to live on" (Mark 12:41-44).

I like this story about the widow's offering because what she gave seems very small and of little value, but it is nonetheless valuable to Christ.

When we give of ourselves to love in the parish, we begin to understand the true value of the two very small copper coins in this story. We become the two small copper coins that Christ recognizes and values as worth more than all the rest. Christ lives through his body in the small things that seem meaningless to almost everyone else. Committing to love our neighborhood seems small, but not to Jesus. It is in the neighborhood where Christ will do his relational, ordinary miracles among us. Most of us do not have eyes to see this. It is too small for our big dreams.

A relational call to love as the body of Christ in the parish seems small, but it's not. Activist Shane Claiborne writes in his book, *The Irresistible Revolution*, that " we live in a world that has lost its appreciation for small things."[1] The small things are hard to value in a culture that craves anything but the small. We think the small will make us seem nonexistent and invisible. We want so much to be noticed that we have taken our life into our own hands and forgotten the small acts of love in the neighborhood. When will we realize that love is the only thing that miracles are made of ? The communal imagination loves the small things in the particulars of everyday life. Our culture has forgotten the true value of two very small copper coins, but we must remember their importance as we live out our lives in the place we inhabit.

"Be faithful in small things," says Mother Teresa, "because it is in them that your strength lies."[2] She goes on to say, "Never think that a small action done to your neighbor is not worth much. It is not how much we do that is pleasing to God, but how much love we put into the doing."[3] And again she says, "For there are many people who can do big things. But there are very few people who will do the small things."[4]

---

[1] Claiborne, *The Irresistible Revolution*, 25.

[2] Mother Teresa, *Everything Starts from Prayer*, 110.

[3] Ibid., 118.

[4] Ibid., 141.

I like Mother Teresa's emphasis on the small. She thought that many people are too big for the small. She thought that North America was the most impoverished continent because we do not know how to love one another, but have everything else. How sad is that?

I have seen the small ways of love that do miracles in my neighborhood. Whenever I see others run into each other and exchange a hug, or listen to each other out of concern for one another, or work alongside each other for the collective good of the neighborhood, or partake in hospitality around a dinner table, I always smile. To me these are small signs of relational miracles taking place before my eyes. I want to be a part of these small things happening in my neighborhood all around me each day. To do so, I must be awake to these relational revelations that come at me like the cool breeze on my face on a summer day.

My friend Nora understands that the small things in everyday life matter so much. She first started to learn this when she was pregnant with her first child, Maggie, several years ago. Our friend Alfredo would give her avocados or put aside soup as a sign of his neighborliness and care. Nora came to realize the extent of Alfredo's care for her family despite the hard time he has speaking English, as his first language is Spanish. Alfredo did the small things that he could do at the time. Alfredo did similar good deeds when Nora was pregnant with her second child, Bridget, a few years later. Alfredo has been a sign to Nora and her husband, Nick, of the small relational ways that God sometimes works.

Nora has been living in the neighborhood for about nine years as a part of the Tacoma Catholic Worker. She has raised her two daughters in the urban context of Downtown Tacoma and sees this as a good thing, even in the midst of the poverty there. Nora does the small things of seeing to it that the place where she lives is safe enough for children, her own and others too. She strives for a peaceful and respectful neighborhood where all people have a voice and are seen even if they are poor and marginalized. Nora embodies a different sense of spirituality to her daughters in which neighbors live out their faith together in everyday life. She is always showing love and belonging to her children through her gentle voice and her affectionate ways.

One day seven-year-old Maggie, Nora's older daughter, came to her asking, "Are there other people who don't have a community that helps others?" Nora looked at her in amazement and just said, "Yes, Maggie, there are people who do not have a loving community that helps others." Then Maggie said, "It's better to help others!" Nora realized that day just how powerfully her lifestyle had impacted Maggie: She had picked up on her embodied expression of spirituality in the neighborhood where Nora is an advocate for the poor, the marginalized, and the hurting in community with others.

Nora loves to work in the neighborhood community garden with her children and others. She feels gardening is something that brings people together in collaboration and friendship, while providing healthier local food sources. For Nora, the community garden is a sacred place of putting our hands in the dirt, playing with children and taking in God's creation on beautiful sunny days.

The garden is a place of imagination, play, picnics, laughter, and friendship. The garden is a place of growth and healing in a lot of ways to our neighborhood. It is sometimes the facilitator of great conversations, parties, and important community events such as weddings and celebrations. The things that might seem to be small to some should never be underestimated in everyday life. They are the vehicles to deep wisdom and relational care among us, as Nora has learned in all kinds of ways.

The small is beautiful. The small is glorious. The small is valuable. The small is strong. The small is countercultural. The small is relevant. The small is ordinary. The small is subversive to the status quo. Artist Luci Shaw has come to the conclusion, "There's a surprising power in small things.[5]" What we think is small is actually really powerful. But it is not always rational . We cannot understand the small just like we cannot always understand Christ. His ways are too "small" for our imaginations. His ways are too "small" for us to control and manipulate. His ways are too "small" to be recognized. We need to embody and "taste" the small as the body of Christ in the parish.

Loving others is all about what the world perceives as too small and too ordinary for it to possibly be of God. Love is not "spiritual" enough for us. Love is not considered "religious" enough for us. Love does not fit into our programs and services. Love cannot be controlled because it is everywhere. Love cannot be boxed up into propositional statements. Love cannot be figured out. Love is relational. Love is mysterious. Love is subversive. Love is countercultural. Love is miraculous.

We are to pay attention to the small, hard-to-see things of life in the parish. "God is love. Whoever lives in love lives in God, and God in him." (I John 4:16). The communal imagination needs eyes for the small. It is through the small that we live our lives. Christ always manifests himself to us through the small. Dorothy Day, co-founder of the Catholic Worker Movement, says in her book *Loaves and Fishes*:

> Young people say, What good can one person do? What is the sense of our small effort? They cannot see that we must lay one brick at a time, take one step at a time; we can be responsible only for the one action of the present moment. But we can beg for an increase of love in our hearts that will vitalize and transform all our individual actions, and know that God will take them and multiply them, as Jesus did the loaves and fishes.[6]

Our love could be multiplied again and again as we do the small things that build relational care in the parish. Are we on a path that will give our lives to explore the small things of love? Jesus is waiting for us in the small particulars of life. He is wanting some collaboration and

---

[5] Shaw, *Breath for the Bones*, 121.

[6] Day, *Loaves and Fishes*, 176.

partnership around the small things where he lives and dwells. "Dear friends, let us love one another, for love comes from God. Everyone who loves has been born of God and knows God. Whoever does not love does not know God, because God is love." (1 John 4:7).

The body of Christ needs to love through the small things that confuse those who all the time want what is bigger and better. We need to embody this communal imagination together in the parish through doing what is small. Our friend, Dwight J. Friesen, Associate Professor of Practical Theology at The Seattle School of Theology and Psychology, points out, "One of the most striking aspects of the good news is the way God seems to delight in using small, insignificant things ... to bring about fantastic transformation."[7]

Making Space in Everyday Life: Investing in the Uniqueness of Others

"Offer hospitality to one another without grumbling..." (1 Peter 4:9). Hospitality has a lot to do with making space for others by being generous with our time. Creating open spaces in our lives in order to connect with others and live relationally is important to the communal imagination. In fact, showing hospitality just might be the holiest thing we could do. We need to do this willingly without grumbling about its demands. The body of Christ needs to make space for others within our lives in the parish. Making space for others fosters love among us. It values our uniqueness. It builds trust and brings value. Without spending time with others there is little relational connection between one another.

"This is the message you heard from the beginning: We should love one another." (1 John 3:11). As we have noted, love is the most valuable expression of human life in the entire universe. Love is the most beautiful miracle in all the world. But without making space for others in our lives, we won't have many chances to show love to one another. We need to become aware of the sacredness of giving our time to make

---

[7] Friesen, *Thy Kingdom Connected*, 142.

space for others in the parish. The body of Christ is called to love in this way in the particulars of everyday life together. Barbara Brown Taylor states, "At its most basic level, the everyday practice of being with other people is the practice of loving the neighbor as the self. More intricately, it is the practice of coming face-to-face with another human being, preferably someone different enough to qualify as the capitol 'O' Other—and at least entertaining the possibility that this is one of the faces of God."[8]

The different faces of God are manifested through our relationships. Our understanding of God is a constant evolving process throughout our entire lives. We learn of God relationally through others in the context of everyday life together. The face-to-face interaction between us manifests relational revelations in the parish. What a wonderful thought that is! I can find Christ in you just as you can find Christ in me. Without being in relationship it is hard to understand Christ in the particulars of everyday life. So we need to make space for one another and be generous with our time. Being with others as a way to demonstrate love could unleash relational miracles just waiting to happen among us.

All of life is about relationship. Without it, we can get lost not knowing who we are. We can only love in relationship. We can only be in relationship by making a hospitable space in our lives for others. Macrina Wiederkehr writes, "I'm not sure of very much in life. I don't have a lot of ready answers, and I still do much wondering and pondering, but there's one thing of which I am certain. We ought not die until we learn to love. Life doesn't work without love."[9] Can life work without relationship? Can life work without love? Can life work without being in a place long enough to have relationship? Can life work if we do not spend the time with others in relationship? So many of us live isolated, lonely lives of our own making. We don't want

---

[8] Taylor, *An Altar in the World*, 94.

[9] Wiederkehr, *A Tree Full of Angels*, 141.

relationship and we choose to live alone and apart from everyone else. How sad to think that so many people live this way.

Making space for others is a better way to live. We will never learn to love if we are not open to others in this way. Love is all good in theory, but it becomes a harsh and dreadful practice in the particulars of everyday life in the parish. Dorothy Day touches on this when she says, "It is too easy to forget that all we give is given to us to give. Nothing is ours. All we have to give is our time and patience, our love."[10]

After about five years of living in Downtown Tacoma, I started to become more curious about the poverty in our parish. I asked myself, "Who are the poor and what are people doing to be in relationship with them in our neighborhood?" I soon learned about the Tacoma Catholic Worker which was a few blocks from where I was living. The community was founded in 1989 when a Jesuit priest named Bill Bichsel, who is now 85 years old, and some other friends wanted to care for those with mental illnesses in the neighborhood. The Catholic Worker consists of eight houses and a big community garden all within one block. Our Downtown Neighborhood Fellowship was (and is) so inspired by their commitment to proximity within the parish and the poor among us!

As I studied the writings of Dorothy Day and New Monastic writers like Shane Claiborne and Jonathan Wilson-Hartgrove, I was so intrigued by their emphasis on hospitality and their understanding of community as a way of life. I wanted to make space in everyday life to be more present to the poor in our neighborhood, to understand their uniqueness and listen to their voices. I was convinced that this is where I would find Christ residing in the lives of the homeless, the poor, the marginalized, the voiceless, the mentally ill, and the addicted. My leadership began to take a new shape as I was drawn to see Christ in the poor in everyday life, to share life with them, to become their friends, to love them and learn their names. What a powerful

---

[10] *Loaves and Fishes*, 177.

movement this was of God in my life, to lead me to care for the poor, to work less so that I could be more present to them by making space within my way of life.

I wanted to be with the poor, so I asked some of my new Catholic Worker friends what I would have to do to become a Catholic Worker. Moving into one of their houses intrigued me a lot. They soon made space for me to practice my faith among the poor in community with them. I moved into one of their houses at the beginning of September 2010.

This has been an amazing experience for me! It is what I believe God had been leading me to and I have found something that resonates deeply within me. The Catholic Workers promote a way of life that is based on simplicity, love, compassion, justice, and hospitality. I have now been at the Catholic Worker for about three years, and I have learned so much from the poor of our neighborhood. Their uniqueness is always speaking to me. Christ is teaching me to follow him by having a more simplistic way of life where I make space within myself for the poor as an act of hospitality. Seeing Christ in the poor in everyday life is helping me to understand what life is without the illusions of escaping what is hard. Our Downtown Neighborhood Fellowship is learning so much about making space in our lives for the poor among us through collaborating with the Tacoma Catholic Worker.

Our time is to be sacrificed for relationship out of love. Our time is not solely ours to choose to waste as each day passes. The communal imagination makes space for others and gives openly of its time. The church is being called to make space for others as an expression of Christ's love in the particulars of everyday life. All we have as the body of Christ is not ours to keep. We need to give to one another our lives out of love. The only thing we can really give to one another is our love in relationship. To be in relationship we need to make space for one another in the parish.

"Dear children, let us not love with words or tongue but with actions and in truth" (1 John 3:18). The actions we need to love in truth have a lot to do with making space for others in our lives. Without making space for others we cannot listen to them, be present with them, see the value and mystery within them, or sacrifice for them. All of this takes time to develop, and we must put a priority on being in relationship like this in the parish. Nothing else will do for the body of Christ in the particulars of everyday life. As Hugh Feiss states so clearly, "If we are too busy to make time for people who need us, whether they are strangers or neighbors, there is something wrong with our priorities."[11] We must not be too busy for others. We must instead allow the communal imagination to set the priorities in our lives together. How tragic when the body of Christ does not have time to be relational in everyday life.

"Dear friends, since God so loved us, we also ought to love one another. No one has ever seen God; but if we love one another, God lives in us and his love is made complete in us" (1 John 4:11-12). Loving one another in the parish entails making space for each other in our own uniqueness. This must become a priority to all in the body of Christ. "To merely welcome another, to provide for him or her, to make a place," Dallas Willard writes, "is one of the most life-giving and life-receiving things a human being can do. They are the basic universal acts of love. Our lives were meant to be full of such acts."[12] The most meaningful thing we can do as the body of Christ is to make space in our lives for others out of love. This is relational and this promotes love. Our lives should be full of love for others as we become an expression of Christ's life here on earth in the place that we share life with others.

Being Nonjudgmental: Practicing Compassion to All

"Show proper respect to everyone" (1 Peter 2:17). We all have the tendency to judge others. But to judge others is to deny them proper

---

[11] Feiss, *Essential Monastic Wisdom*, 5.

[12] Willard, *Renovation of the Heart*, 183.

respect. When we judge one another we discriminate against ourselves and lose our hold on love. Judging others hinders us from loving others. "Above all, love each other deeply" (1 Peter 4:8). We need to love as the body of Christ, not judge. Judging others tends to be the religious thing to do nowadays. We don't want to get caught up in all this religious stuff. Instead, we want to love others in a contextual way within the particulars of everyday life in the parish.

Judging others does more damage than we sometimes realize. The communal imagination doesn't judge others but loves them compassionately.

> Do not judge, or you too will judged. For in the same way you judge others, you will be judged, and with the measure you use, it will be measured to you.

> Why do you look at the speck of sawdust in your brother's eye and pay no attention to the plank in your own eye? How can you say to your brother, 'Let me take the speck out of your eye,' when all the time there is a plank in your own eye? You hypocrite, first take the plank out of your own eye, and then you will see clearly to remove the speck from your brother's eye. (Matthew 7:1-5).

It is very clear that Christ does not want the members of his body going around judging everyone. Bruxy Cavey states, "Jesus promoted a nonjudgmental spirituality ... Those who follow Jesus are called to represent God's love to others, but not his judgment."[13] This "nonjudgmental spirituality" communicates love relationally. Christ calls us to love, not to judge. We all would rather be loved than judged. This is a common human experience. Judging others keeps us from listening and being present in relationship. Judging others keeps us from practicing compassion. And compassion is at the heart of spirituality. Christ's love is what we want to express with our lives, not a judgmental attitude that robs us of anything authentic.

---

[13] Cavey, *The End of Religion*, 213.

It is so easy to judge and much harder to embody love toward others. If we are to learn to love we have to let go of our need to judge others. Judging others is violent and cruel. It is devaluing and not liberating. It gives us control over those we judge. It is safe and predictable. It demands nothing of us. It is boring and uncreative. But love is more powerful than judgment. It overcomes its power to devalue and control, and helps us to become alive and free.

"And this is his command: to believe in the name of his Son, Jesus Christ, and to love one another as he commanded us" (1 John 3:23). When we love we become nonjudgmental. How freeing it is not to judge others and to demonstrate our love in our local context. Christ is leading us to take on this nonjudgmental attitude and learn to love in the place we inhabit together. It has a lot to do with walking in the Spirit and practicing compassion. We are chained to our ego when we judge. There is real liberation when we love together as the body of Christ in the parish. It can liberate our imaginations and free us to be more communal.

We limit our love when we judge. It can even become an addiction if we are not careful. No one usually considers judging others an addiction. But I believe it can become one. We have addictions to all kinds of things that do damage to ourselves, but we usually don't see judging others in that light. Yet to me, judging others is a very common addiction that causes us to live outside of relationship in everyday life. How can we be in relationship with others when we are always judging them? This is not healthy. It does constant damage to us and to those we share life with. We become less than human when we replace love with judgment. The body of Christ is called to lay down its judgment and learn to love others in the parish. Dietrich Bonhoeffer writes, "Judging others makes us blind, whereas love is illuminating."[14]

One day I was walking in Downtown Tacoma, I saw a man standing there on the corner of 11th and Tacoma Ave. yelling at the top of his

---

[14] Bonhoeffer, *The Cost of Discipleship*, 185.

voice, "I hate people!" He was a person whom I had never seen before. He was obviously in a lot of pain. He might have been a man from the shelter down the street, but I really didn't know for sure. My first thought was to judge this man for expressing his hatred so openly. Then I felt a sense of compassion for the man. Thoughts started to run through my head: "Where was he from? What was his story? How had he been devalued in his life? What are his broken dreams? Is he lonely? Who are his friends and family?"

I happened to be walking on the other side of the street while all of this was going on and never approached the man. Not knowing what to do, I felt sad that I was seeing someone with so much pain in his life right there in front of me. I wanted to ignore the whole thing, but it was practically impossible. It was hard to escape. Feeling there was nothing I could do, I just kept walking until I was far enough away that I could no longer hear his voice anymore. My questions were never answered that day as to what had happened to this man and I never saw him again. I just walked away from his screaming voice kind of startled and afraid because of my discomfort in the whole situation. I didn't realize it at the time, but God was revealing something very important within me.

Every time I walk by the corner of 11th and Tacoma Ave., God moves me to new depths of solidarity and compassion. This corner of our parish has become a sacramental monument to me of the suffering, the lonely, and the devalued of our society who feel hatred, betrayal and anything but love. I oftentimes weep at the thought that so many in the parish where I live experience this kind of suffering and poverty. I am learning not to hold onto my judgmental attitudes of those who have different stories of suffering than what I can relate to. God is teaching me compassion, especially to the poor, and moving me to become an expression of love in the midst of the pain and suffering of some of our neighbors in everyday life.

We tend to judge because we want everyone to be the same. We want life to be controlled and not messy. We want others to be like us. When they are different from us we do not know what to do with them, so we judge them instead of showing love. But the reality is that we are all so different. We cannot be expected to be the same. Even Christians are all so different from one another. We all have unique personalities and preferences that make us who we are. That might bother some of us, but we are wise if we will see that this is just the way life is. Diversity is a good thing when we learn to love. Others don't have to be the same as me. "Without embracing the truth that it is okay to be different," says spiritual director Alice Fryling in her book *Seeking God Together*, "we may indeed be quick to judge each other."[15]

When we love as the body of Christ in the particulars of everyday life together we will stop judging others. We will not understand the language of judgment so much and will lean toward a more inclusive way of love. Loving our neighbor will be taken out of the abstract and placed right in front of us in the parish. We will be shaped by practicing this love and compassion to all.

"Therefore let us stop passing judgment on one another" (Romans 14:13). When we judge others as the body of Christ we lose touch with the relational. All of life is relational when we are led and guided by love. Our judgments do not lead and guide us in the particulars of everyday life. As Richard Rohr says, "when we lead off with our judgments, love will seldom happen ..."[16] A judgmental attitude will shut down life within us. Love must lead the body of Christ. We do not inhabit a place properly with judgment living in our bones.

I have had such a long journey of learning how to love and not judge as I live in my neighborhood. People are different from me. But God says to me, "So what, does that excuse you from loving them?" I would have to answer, "No, not really." There is no excuse that I can give to God that will lead me to judge instead of love. The Spirit always leads me to love and never leads me to judge. I am slowly coming to understand

---

[15] Fryling, *Seeking God Together*, 102.

[16] Rohr, *Things Hidden*, 38.

this more. I can allow God to help me with my addiction to judge and learn to live with a more intuitive love for the others around me. Relationship can happen in no other way. I have experienced many relational revelations when I love instead of judge. Christ is the One who personifies love and not judgment. I am coming to embody this aspect of Christ more in my life and am learning how to love within the context of everyday life in, with, and for my community.

"Let no doubt remain outstanding, except the continuing debt to love on another, for he who loves his fellowman has fulfilled the law ... Love does no harm to its neighbor. Therefore love is the fulfillment of the law" (Romans 13:8,10). Love is the fulfillment of the law, not judgment. The body of Christ needs to love in everyday life together in the parish. When we do this, judgment slowly becomes more foreign within our relationships. We start to learn to love and practice compassion. We begin to notice all kinds of relational revelations happening in the context of ordinary everyday life. They sneak up on us sometimes without our really knowing what is happening. But over time, wisdom is revealing herself to us. Love will never harm a relationship, but will strengthen it. Judgment will always damage a relationship. The communal imagination always embraces this kind of love.

Part 3

Becoming an Expression of Grace: Learning to be Human Again

Chapter 6

Facing One Another in Everyday Life: The Path to Healing and Growth

Relational Flexibility: Embracing Ideals and then Letting them Go

Several years ago, I had the opportunity to spend some time with Shane Claiborne down in Alabama at a Lent retreat. Typically, Shane speaks in front of at least five hundred people when he shares, but this weekend was different because there was a tornado warning on the day he arrived and only about twenty people showed up because of it. I had never been to Alabama before, so to experience tornado sirens go off on the first evening of the retreat was interesting to say the least. But because there were so few of us, I got to spend some good one-on-one time with him. I ate breakfast, lunch and dinner next to him at the same table for several days. Previously, I had read some of Shane's books like *The Irresistible Revolution* which had had a dramatic influence on me. So I really appreciated all the conversation that I got a chance to have with him that weekend. I was really excited. I had a hundred questions for him. Back home, I am known for asking many questions and sometimes wearing others out if they are not in the mood for it.

After many hours of conversation with Shane, I remember asking him what he thought was the most challenging thing he had learned about living in community in his neighborhood of Kensington, Philadelphia at The Simple Way for the past fifteen years or so. I will never forget what he told me that day. He said the most important thing he had learned was that learning to love his community unconditionally is so much more important than getting caught up in the ideals of what he thinks the community should be.

I thought this was such profound wisdom and I'm thankful for having the chance to spend some time with him that weekend. I have been inspired by Shane for many years through his books, so having the chance to hear him in person say these words to me was very powerful. This conversation has had a profound influence on me to this day. His words have always stayed with me and I think about them often. Dietrich Bonhoeffer says in his insightful book *Life Together*, "Innumerable times a whole Christian community has broken down because it had sprung from a wish dream. The serious Christian, set down for the first time in a Christian community, is likely to bring with him a very definite idea of what Christian life together should be and to try to realize it. But God's grace speedily shatters such dreams."[1]

Bonhoeffer goes on to say,

> By sheer grace, God will not permit us to live even for a brief period in a dream world. He does not abandon us to those rapturous experiences and lofty moods that come over us like a dream ... Only that fellowship which faces such disillusionment, with all its unhappy and ugly aspects, begins to be what it should be in God's sight, begins to grasp in faith the promise that is given to it. The sooner this shock of disillusionment comes to an individual and to a community the better for both. A community which cannot bear and cannot survive such a crisis, which insists upon keeping its illusion when it should be shattered, permanently loses in that moment the promise of Christian community. Sooner or later it will collapse. Every human wish dream that is injected into the Christian community is a hindrance to genuine community and must be banished if genuine community is to

---

[1] Bonhoeffer, *Life Together*, 26-27.

survive. He who loves his dream of community more than the Christian community itself becomes a destroyer of the latter, even though his personal intentions may be ever so honest and earnest and sacrificial.[2]

We always face a great tension between the ideal of what we want life to be like and the reality of life as it is. The communal imagination is not built on a "wish dream" or an illusion, but on reality. We will struggle sometimes to figure things out relationally in the parish. It is not always easy and we might often fail. But we need to keep trying to learn to live with grace towards one another. Without grace, we will build our lives on a lofty illusion of how things ought to be with little contact with reality. What we are building will not last very long without grace. When we love our ideals of community more than the reality of the community, we will become disillusioned and bring an oppressive agenda into it that will quickly poison everything around us.

I have been caught up in this for many years. When I first moved to Downtown Tacoma, I was sure that my friends and I were going to do amazing things together and have much influence. But after a while, things weren't really working out the way I had hoped. My ideals soared through the sky, but after the first few years it seemed nothing much was happening. I struggled with depression, anger and fear that I had thrown my life away on something that was not really possible. How could we create a culture of relational connection in the neighborhood and share life together when we were having such a hard time with one another? A lot of us did not have the relational skills necessary to live out the gospel in our locality. So I just complained a lot and hoped for something to change. But I have realized that my ideals cannot lead my life anymore. I have to live for what is. I have to be a person of imagination and passion without being attached to ideals and outcomes. I have to allow myself to be shaped by my relational context. This has been one of the most pressing demands on my life as I share life with my friends in the parish.

---

[2] Ibid., 27.

Not that I have already obtained all this, or have already been made perfect, but I press on to take hold of that for which Christ Jesus took hold of me. Brothers, I do not consider myself yet to have taken hold of it. But one thing I do: Forgetting what is behind and straining toward what is ahead, I press on toward the goal to win the prize for which God has called me heavenward in Christ Jesus.

All of us who are mature should take such a view of things. And if on some point you think differently, that too God will make clear to you. Only let us live up to what we have already obtained.

Join with others in following my example, brothers, and take note of those who live according to the pattern we gave you" (Philippians 3:12-17).

Paul was grounded in reality and not caught up in his ideals. What was the goal he was pressing on to achieve? Maybe it was the goal of being in relationship with others as a way of being in relationship with God. He wanted to become an expression of God's grace to the church in Philippi. He wanted to continue on with his relationship with them after he got out of prison. Paul thought that the only way to win the prize was to know God through others relationally. He was torn about being away from them. He had great hope for their lives. He encourages the Philippians to live up to what they have already attained. They must have attained to a grace for one another in their locality that made relational revelations possible in their community. He was encouraging them to keep pursuing this and to consider his example when he was among them. He wanted them to take note of those among them who demonstrated a relational grace through his example.

I thank God every time I remember you. In all my prayers for all of you, I always pray with joy because of your partnership in the gospel from the first day until now, being confident of this, that he who began a good work in you will carry it on to completion until the day of Christ Jesus.

It is right for me to feel this way about all of you, since I have you in my heart; for whether I am in chains defending or confirming the gospel, all of you share in God's grace with me. God can testify how I long for all of you with the affection of Christ Jesus" (Philippians 1:3-8).

Paul is affirming his desire to be in relationship with the Philippians. He is longing for this just as he longs for Christ. This is not based on some idealized illusion, but on the reality of relationship. They have been partnering and sharing in becoming expressions of God's grace in their locality. Paul tells them that God will continue to do this work within them all. He urges them to continue on with all of this.

The body of Christ is called to live into its place without being attached to seemingly "good" ideals that can become dangerous and damaging to our relationships. We need to learn from Bonhoeffer's words and Paul's relationship with the Philippians. These can teach us how to be in relationship with others without getting caught up in ideals. Our ideals can keep us from the grace that must be a part of our lives together in the particulars of everyday life. We all have to go through the filtering of our ideals to come into the reality of real relationship. Our ideals cannot blind us any longer in the parish. The communal imagination is too important for us to allow our ideals to destroy it.

We are all called to become an expression of grace in the place we inhabit together. We will not function properly without grace. Grace is healing to our relationships. Grace is what will make it possible to share life together in the particulars of everyday life. Illusions, ideals, and "wish dreams" will not take us very far together. We need not get caught up in all of this. The reality of our relationships is often very different than what we may have envisioned them to be at the outset. Relationships are unpredictable. They are messy. They teach us constantly to show grace and love. We cannot escape the grace of relationship. If we do, we become isolated and extremely lonely. There is nothing to do and nowhere to go except to face one another with grace. This will help us to learn to be the body of Christ. "Many times we are driven by an illusion," Annemarie S. Kidder says, "of what true

Christian community should look like, chasing after a dream and being disappointed by the realities."[3]

Grace stems from our love for others. "Be patient, bearing with one another in love" (Ephesians 4:2). We need to have patience and grace for one another as expressions of our love for one another . Without this our ideals will take over and ruin us. Our relationships will not be sustainable. And we will soon forget about one another and our local context. In his book *A Hidden Wholeness*, Parker J. Palmer writes, "In particular, we must learn to hold the tension between the reality of the moment and the possibility that something better might emerge."[4] We have to understand the balancing act of the reality and the potential of everyday life together in the parish. The reality is sometimes hard to face. The potential gives us great hope. So we need to live inside of this tension. This is one of the ways we learn to lay down our lives as the body of Christ and allow God to enlighten us. This is a mystery that only God can teach us through practicing relationship.

I have struggled so much with this tension between the real and the possible. Sometimes I become depressed and want it all to go away. But this is the process of life that I must face as I journey with the body of Christ in everyday life. I cannot make it go away, but that is okay. I am learning to not get caught up in all the illusions. I realize that at times our grace will be challenged. Sometimes it all seems impossible. But God has been forming a communal imagination in my neighborhood that is full of possibilities and potential. My friends and I want to continue to be an expression of grace together as we learn how to be in relationship with each other. The Spirit is working everyday to manifest relational revelations through us all. I am continually learning that grace is a miracle we can all become a part of through relationship.

"I want you to know how much I am struggling for you" (Colossians 2:1). Paul is struggling for the people of Colossae without getting

---

[3] Kidder, *The Power of Solitude*, 22.

[4] Palmer, *A Hidden Wholeness*, 175.

caught up in his ideals versus the reality of his relationship with them. Paul in his letters is always very relational and inspirational to the communities he is seeking to encourage. He desires to be a channel of God's grace to each one of his friends, whether they be in Colossae, Philippi, Corinth or Ephesus. Paul wants us to follow his example as he follows the example of Christ. He wants us to become channels of grace towards one another through relationship, so that the body of Christ can be seen in the local contexts of everyday life. Dwight J. Friesen writes, "Glorious surprises and unforeseen tragedies have a way of bringing order and chaos into relationships, often changing the course of our existence. Fullness of life is not embracing the glorious while sidestepping the tragedies; rather fullness of life is saying yes to God's invitation to fullness in and through embracing the dance of both the tragedies and the glories."[5]

We never know what will surface as we interact with one another in our neighborhood, but we must be willing to engage with grace the life we find there. "Glories" and "tragedies" will manifest themselves all around us all the time. So we must find a posture of grace in our relationships that does not get overly focused on the glorious "wish dreams" to the exclusion of the unpredictable tragedies in life. Grace will guide and protect our relationships from self-destruction as we live out our lives together in the parish.

Community is not about ideals, but about real people who live in a real place. Ideals can mask reality. We should be aware of this and hope to become expressions of grace within our reality. Life is messy, and we don't always have the neatest experience all of the time. But it is the relationships that we have in our locality that make us who we are. Our relationships are our greatest teachers. They always have something to teach us in everyday life. The body of Christ is made up of nothing else but our relationships. We should not see our relationships as drawing us away from experiencing life, but as a help and a guide for us to embrace

---

[5] Friesen, *Thy Kingdom Connected*, 95.

life. It is always through the relational that Christ lives through his body in the parish.

The communal imagination needs some flexibility and openness to navigate around the ideals we bring into our lives together. The body of Christ needs to live in grace for others through our relational encounters each day. Our ideals are oftentimes dogmatic, acontextual, and overly religious. Quite frankly, they are not helpful most of the time and can cause great damage to us relationally. But we must fight to hold onto the reality of our relationships. We need to become expressions of grace to one another and see that as most important. "Openness challenges us," John O' Keefe says, "to move past the dogmatic, the doctrinal, the religious and into the open arms of the divine grace that should define us as followers."[6] God's grace and love should lead us as followers of Christ in the parish. Nothing else has the power to shape us and sustain into the future. When we become open to the reality of our relationships without becoming overly attached to the possibility of our ideals, then we can begin to be the body of Christ together in everyday life. The parish will be the medium where grace is manifested to us all.

Learning to Face One Another without Fear: The Context of Belonging

Why is it so hard to face one another in life? We like to hide. We do not like to be in relationship a lot of the time. Yet the communal imagination is calling us to be in relationship with one another learning how to face one another without the many fears that plague us. We like to run from one another because it is easier than running towards one another. But this is not what the body of Christ is called to in our local context. We will need to learn how to face those we live with and not back away from grace. Grace will show us how to do this. We need to have the imagination for something more creative than relationships that are ego-centered and dysfunctional. This is the context for

---

[6] O' Keefe, *BoneYARD*, 118.

belonging. God has given us so much more that has still to be discovered in the parish. We need one another to teach us grace.

We are called to live in a state of constant reconciliation with others in everyday life. This is so important if we are to become an expression of grace together. Grace and reconciliation are intertwined into a constant living reality through the difficult work of living together in the parish. We have to see the need and the provision that God has given to us by his own grace. The body of Christ will become the living expression of grace and reconciliation as we live into the communal imagination. When we can live in grace, then we can face one another in life. This will bring healing to our relationships. This healing in turn will help cultivate our sustainability in the place we live. "And he has committed us to the message of reconciliation. We are therefore Christ's ambassadors, as though God were making his appeal through us" (2 Corinthians 5:19-20). We need reconciliation and grace to be able to face one another without fear. This is how we become Christ's ambassadors. This is how we represent the communal imagination among us. This is how Christ lives through us in the parish.

Our spirituality has everything to do with facing one another through relationship. All our relationships should become drenched with grace. Grace is the way we are to be in relationship with one another. How can we face one another in any other way? If there is little grace in our relationships, we will not be able to face one another very well. We will constantly fail without grace for others. Ronald Rolheiser states, "Hence a Christian spirituality is always as much about dealing with each other as it is about dealing with God."[7] Our Christianity is to be embraced among others through becoming an expression of grace in the parish. We need to be in relationship with one another through grace in order to face one another without fear.

Sometimes we run from relationships because there is no grace and we are afraid of one another. Without having grace to face one another we

---

[7] Rolheiser, *The Holy Longing*, 99.

do not have much. When we do not have much, our relationships fall apart. We become disillusioned with the body of Christ in the process. Our whole society counsels us to run away from relationships. From when we were very young, almost everything in life has taught us to run away. Our mobility, wealth and technology allow us to escape our local context. We do not have to face one another anymore if we do not choose to. When things get hard in relationships, we usually just leave them and pick up life somewhere else. We think this is freedom, but it is really anything but that. How can we learn to live in reconciliation and grace facing one another in the particulars of everyday life if all we do is run away from life's problems? We must work out our salvation together in the parish and strive to figure it out. The communal imagination calls us to nothing less.

My friend Justin has been living in our neighborhood for about six years now. He has become a good friend to many people in our local context, but it has been a struggle for him to face his fears of entering into relationships. Justin has lived in a co-housing situation for most of his time in the neighborhood and is soon moving into the Guadalupe house of the Tacoma Catholic Worker. Facing himself and others in vulnerability has been one of Justin's hardest challenges. He has really worked at figuring out stuff about himself and being okay with those who are different from him. Interacting with others in spite of their differences has been important to his life in the parish. Justin is constantly unlearning the individualism that he had been taught through his family of origin and cultural context.

Within Justin there has been a transformation. He can now imagine an alternate way of life where he can find belonging through learning to face others in everyday life without fear. He has been accepted by many people in his relational context and this has been healing for him. Justin has been in the process of discovering and understanding more about himself which has contributed to his experience of God in the place where he lives. His rootedness has taught him to face others and just be himself while allowing the relational context to shape him in everyday life.

Sometimes Justin is not the most involved person in our neighborhood. He can be anti-social, but he is still accepted. Others have believed in Justin as he has struggled to find himself through it all. Gratitude and belonging have been crucial in Justin's journey towards life without fear. He is learning to see the commonalities among his neighbors instead of the differences between them, which has made this process of sharing life with others much easier at times. There are three children in our community, Colletta, Bridget and Lincoln, who just love Justin. Theirs is just one example of the kindness, love, and grace that Justin has shown to so many in our neighborhood. Justin has practiced the courage to face others in everyday life. We have all seen the fruit of his love and grace for others. It encourages all of us who have come to know Justin as a friend.

"You then, my son, be strong in the grace that is in Christ Jesus" (2 Timothy 2:1). We are to live into the grace that is in Christ and learn to become expressions of that grace together. We need to face one another in everyday life and learn to live relationally in, through, and by grace. Grace must be allowed to have a profound presence in all we do and hold our very existence in balance. We must not forget how to face one another in the parish. "Carry each other's burdens, and in this way you will fulfill the law of Christ" (Galatians 6:2). We carry each other through grace. We carry each other by learning to face one another.

This can be extremely hard. I have often found myself running and hiding from relationship with others. Relationships often break me down, test my limits, and shape who I am becoming. I have to learn how to face the reality of the other. This always becomes a reflection of my own weakness and causes me to see life differently, to see God differently. My whole world changes in the process of facing the other.

When we learn how to face one another, we become a powerful expression of grace. To be in relationship is to be shaped by our faithful presence. Many of us do not like this process, so we stay far away from one another. When we do this, we reject the practice of facing one another. And we cease to be the body of Christ in everyday life. When others hurt us, it is hard to have to continually face them again and again. But we must learn to show grace and be present in face-to-face relationship day by day. We must never turn our backs on others. We need to become expressions of grace in the midst of our pain. We must constantly be open to one another in grace. We must constantly allow God to do relational miracles among us as we learn to face one another in the parish.

We need to recover our humanity and embrace one another face to face. We are more connected to one another than we sometimes realize. We need to live into that connection through grace and not run from one another. The relationships that we share together will shape us as we take a posture of grace toward one another. "We have no real being 'until we have faces' to receive the other, to offer ourselves, and then to pass on our very selves in the same way," says Richard Rohr. "It will be experienced as depth, acceptance and forgiveness for being who we are, a quality of being that is shared, compassionate and totally gift."[8]

> Let us hold unswervingly to the hope we profess, for he who promised is faithful. And let us consider how we may spur one another on toward love and good deeds. Let us not give up meeting together, as some are in the habit of doing, but let us encourage one another—and all the more as you see the Day approaching (Hebrews 10:23-25).

Many have understood this passage to be about not giving up on meeting together in a building for a weekly worship service. But maybe this passage is about something totally different. When the writer is talking about meeting together, it's possible this refers to living together in a place. The writer could be saying to not give up facing one another in the day-to-day of life. If so, then the writer is communicating that we need to continually meet together and share life in the particulars of everyday life in our local context. The word "meet" in Greek has connotations of togetherness, relationship, reconciliation, shared life,

---

[8] Rohr, *Things Hidden*, 67.

collaboration and partnership. We need to meet together on the streets. We need to meet together in public spaces such as parks, coffee shops and restaurants. We need to meet together in gardens and studios. We need to meet together in each other's homes. We need to meet together in dialogue and meaningful conversation. We need to meet together in contemplation. We need to meet together in face-to-face relationship in the parish.

This rendering of this passage in Hebrews seems more holistic. It is not just about where we meet together and what we do, but it is also about how we meet together relationally. We always must approach our meeting together with a posture of grace towards one another. This is the communal imagination at its best.

Our Downtown Neighborhood Fellowship has had times where we couldn't face one another in grace very well. We have been immature at times and have had trouble getting along. We have had trouble relating with each other in our diversity. We have had trouble learning to follow Christ in our relationships with one another.

I have known some of my friends in the neighborhood now for ten years or so, and we have a lot of history together. It has been hard for us to constantly show grace to one another. But we are doing our best. We are learning that the gospel is all talk if we can't even get along and become expressions of grace. In the future, our relationships will be tested to see if we can live in grace for one another. God is using our neighborhood of Downtown Tacoma to constantly reveal to us relationally how to live together, share life together, show grace together, and learn to face one another. These are where the ordinary miracles in everyday life begin among us.

Marius Grout says, "By your capacity for forgiveness shall I recognize your God."[9] Forgiveness is an ordinary miracle and is the path of following Christ through our relationships. Forgiveness makes us receptive to the life of God within us. Without forgiveness we lose our humanity. We end up living a miserable existence without relationship to one another. We become isolated from relationship. Without forgiveness we have nothing. Without forgiveness the body of Christ becomes irrelevant to its local context. What a tragedy when we live out of something else besides forgiveness. Our relationships are created and sustained through our forgiveness for one another. We will hurt each other over and over again. But we have to decide if we will live in forgiveness or opt out of relationship altogether .

> Then Peter came to Jesus and asked, "Lord, how many times shall I forgive my brother when he sins against me? Up to seven times?"
>
> Jesus answered, "I tell you not seven times, but seventy-seven times.
>
> Therefore, the kingdom of heaven is like a king who wanted to settle accounts with his servants. As he began the settlement, a man who owed him ten thousand talents was brought to him. Since he was not able to pay, the master ordered that he and his wife and his children and all that he had be sold to repay the debt.
>
> The servant fell on his knees before him. 'Be patient with me,' he begged, 'and I will pay back everything.' The servant's master took pity on him, canceled the debt and let him go.
>
> But when the servant went out, he found one of his fellow servants who owed him a hundred denarii. He grabbed him and began to choke him. 'Pay back what you owe me!' he demanded.
>
> His fellow servant fell to his knees and begged him, 'Be patient with me, and I will pay you back.'

---

[9] Grout, "Growing Together," 159.

'But he refused. Instead, he went off and had the man thrown into prison until he could pay the debt. When the other servants saw what had happened, they were greatly distressed and went and told their master everything that had happened.

Then the master called the servant in. 'You wicked servant,' he said, 'I canceled all that debt of yours because you begged me to. Shouldn't you have had mercy on your fellow servant just as I had on you?' In anger his master turned him over to the jailers to be tortured, until he should pay back all he owed.

This is how my heavenly Father will treat each of you unless you forgive your brother from your heart" (Matthew 18:21-35).

Jesus is teaching us to forgive the amount of seven times seventy. If you do the math, this is 490 times. He is stressing that forgiveness is so important to our relationships. How can we forgive each other 490 times, if we are not in the kind of relationships that allow us to be around each other that much? If we were around each other a bare minimum of just once a week, it would take us about nine and a half years to be around each other 490 times. Some of us do not even stay in the same place long enough to see 490 relational encounters take place. If we were around each other three times a week, it would still take about three-and-a-half years to be around each other 490 times. If we were around each other almost every day, it would take about a year and a half. And out of all those encounters, there will be some where we don't actually forgive or don't have to forgive. And that makes us need more relational encounters to forgive 490 times. It could take us up to ten to twenty years to actually forgive 490 times. The point to all of this is that we need to have an ongoing posture of forgiveness and grace toward one another all throughout our lives together in the parish as the body of Christ.

We should be a forgiving people. This is how we walk in the Spirit. This is how Christ lives through his body. Christ longs to bring forgiveness and reconciliation into the world through our relationships with one another in the parish. How mysterious and strange this is, but Christ always works through the particulars of our relationships.

Martin Luther King Jr. writes, "A man cannot forgive up to four hundred and ninety times without forgiveness becoming a part of the habit structure of his being. Forgiveness is not an occasional act; it is a permanent attitude."[10] We need to approach life with a paradigm of forgiveness and grace in all that we do. Almost everything in life wants to pull us away from this kind of forgiveness. Society wants to keep us apart. Because when we live disconnected, ungraceful lives, we will have to depend more upon centralized systems that have little concern for our relational connections. Forgiveness needs to become "a permanent attitude" within our relationships. Nothing else will do for the communal imagination.

My friend Holly is such a great example of forgiveness in Downtown Tacoma. As she has embraced this place as her home, she has found forgiveness to be just as much for herself as for others. By running into people everyday, Holly has learned to face her resentments. She has noticed that there are tensions within her when she lives in unforgiveness towards someone in her life. God has been showing her that forgiveness is necessary for ongoing friendships with neighbors. When a rift happens in her relationships she doesn't hide from that; but she has realized that forgiveness requires of her intention, thought, and communication. Holly has learned that it is okay to be angry sometimes, creating boundaries and distance if necessary with some added structure in difficult times in her relationships.

After many years of living in the parish, Holly has experienced injustices that are not okay with her. She has learned to love herself despite tensions and difficulties when the pain was too much. Forgiveness takes times and sometimes Holly has had to be graceful with herself in the struggle. It has been difficult for her to just forgive automatically and throw things off as if they have never happened, but Holly is allowing God to shape her through this process. Forgiveness requires learning through practice, and an emotional healing that can sometimes be hard to achieve. Hiding is not something that Holly

---

10 King Jr., *Strength to Love*, 37-38.

wants for herself or her friends in the neighborhood. She practices facing others with grace and forgiveness. It has transformed her life. This has been important for Holly to address in her own life with others. She's seen that resentments always create more resentments which are never helpful. Now Holly hopes for so much more from others. She hopes for a communal imagination built around forgiveness and life rather than resentments.

Taking responsibility for her part of the relationship is something Holly is learning to do. She cannot escape it. Every relationship has at least two pieces to it, so we need to take responsibility for our part. Holly has learned the vulnerability it takes to do the work of forgiveness. She has learned not to live with a victim mentality, but instead to always make choices that sustain a different way of life. Self-responsibility has shown Holly to live in her own story and to show up with courage to do the things that God is calling her to.

Christ was a forgiver. Christ still is a forgiver. Christ lived in grace. Christ still lives in grace. The body of Christ needs to learn of him in this way. We need to learn to forgive. We need to learn to become an expression of his grace to one another in our relationships in the parish. This is the only sustainable way to live out our lives together. Forgiveness is the only way we can sustain our relational connections to one another. Living in proximity is impossible without forgiveness. It is just too hard and we will not have the strength to get along without grace and forgiveness. Our relationships will fall apart and become an illusion without forgiveness. We need to open ourselves up to Christ through forgiveness toward one another. Christ is manifested to us through our forgiveness. If we don't get this, the communal imagination will not have a chance to live in and among us. Could embracing a holistic spirituality among us be wrapped up in the way we forgive one another? Trappist mystic Thomas Merton states, "It is our forgiveness of one another that makes the love of Jesus for us manifest in our lives, for in forgiving one another we act towards one another as He acted towards us."[11]

We cannot share life together in the parish without this gift of forgiveness and grace infusing our relationships. We like to talk about God's grace in terms of our own forgiveness, but when will we shift to a new paradigm of translating that grace into our deepest conflicts and struggles to love one another? This would be a miracle indeed.

Sometimes the last thing we want to do is forgive each other, live together, share some life together. Running away from one another makes forgiveness impossible and damages the body of Christ. We need to have the courage to be in relationship with one another and to forgive over and over again. This would lighten our egocentric agendas and cause us to lose control of our lives. We would have to depend more on the Spirit than our own egos. There will be times we won't like this, but it is an essential relational discipline that will cultivate our relationships with one another. Without forgiveness we cease to live. We die and grow dysfunctional, existing but not truly alive. Without grace and forgiveness, we can become extremely mean and cruel and ugly to one another. In their fantastic book *The Abundant Community* John McKnight and Peter Block say, "In community, we cannot run from our history together. Forgiveness is required when we have to live together."[12] We need to wake up to this call on our lives together in the parish.

"Bear with each other and forgive whatever grievances you may have against one another" (Colossians 3:13). We need to live into the communal imagination and learn to how to forgive. We are not very good at this. There needs to be more practice around what forgiveness actually looks like in the local context where we live. Bearing with each other is hard work and will test all our ideas of the power of the gospel. If we can't live in forgiveness, how true is the message of the gospel to

---

[11] Merton, *Thoughts in Solitude*, 37.

[12] McKnight and Block, *The Abundant Community*, 88.

us? This moves everything out of just propositional statements and into real life. This is how we are to live in our relationships to one another. We may say that is impossible, but listen to the words of Philippians 4:13: "I can do everything through him who gives me strength." Paul is saying that we can live a life of forgiveness and grace toward one another because it is Christ who is our strength. And we can do everything that is required of us through a strength that is not our own. Christ is powerful and so is the message of the gospel of God's grace.

I must say that forgiveness has been the one thing that has seemed impossible over the years that I have lived in my neighborhood. In many struggles, challenges, and tensions, I have not always had kind words to say to others. But I am learning how to be in relationship with my neighbors in a way that is pleasant, graceful, and forgiving. I don't want to hate and disregard others anymore. Working through differences and disagreements is something that has been pushing me to embody empathy and forgiveness toward others when necessary. I have to allow myself to become hurt at times, and to open myself up to others regardless. This is the challenging call of Christ on my life. Sometimes I don't want to forgive as Christ forgives us. I tell myself, "That is all good in theory, but not in real life." And yet so much of our Christianity is only theory. When will we learn to put into practice the things Jesus taught us with those we share life with?

"Be kind and compassionate to one another, forgiving each other, just as in Christ God forgave you" (Ephesians 4:32). The communal imagination forgives. This is not optional. This is the way of the body of Christ. The body of Christ will die without forgiveness towards one another. We need to become expressions of forgiveness to one another in the neighborhood we inhabit. This will manifest the body of Christ to others in our particular locality. If we cannot forgive, we have nothing to offer to ourselves or to anyone else. We will embarrass ourselves and give out a message of unbelief concerning the very thing we are claiming to believe. "If it is possible, as far as it depends on you, live at peace with everyone. Do not take revenge, my friends" (Romans 12:18-19). If we cannot forgive, we cannot live a peaceful life with one another. We will constantly fight for our own agendas. And if things don't go our way, we will soon choose to leave the neighborhood altogether. This is tragic and sad. Forgiveness is so much more the better option. It is holistic and kind. It is filled with relational revelations and social capital.

Everything is interconnected with our ability to forgive others. Community is only possible when forgiveness is alive within the body of Christ in the parish. We would never be able to get along without forgiveness. It is the foundation for all relational revelations and ordinary miracles in everyday life. It sustains life. It is as essential as eating and sleeping. We all feel valued when we are forgiven and others show us some grace. There should be no escaping this grace towards one another. Without forgiveness our spirits die and we become less than human. We start to lose our understanding of what it means to be made in God's image and instead become driven by our own agendas and egos. Influential author Henri Nouwen says, "It's so important that we keep forgiving one another—not once in a while but every moment of life. This is what makes community possible, when we come together in a forgiving and undemanding way."[13]

Our Downtown Neighborhood Fellowship has experienced much pain over the years and we have not always done a good job at getting along and forgiving one another. There have been times where we have had to work through our hurt and didn't really want to share life anymore with one another. We have had to decide over and over again whether we are going to be committed to one another, working through our differences, or move on and live individualistic lives. Are we going to forget our commitment to the neighborhood and to one another? This has been an imposing question for us in Downtown Tacoma. How can we forgive one another and be in relationship with one another? How can we create a life here in the midst of our pain?

---

[13] Nouwen, *Spiritual Direction*, 119.

I don't know that we have it all figured out, but we are on our way to living these questions through the good and bad times of our lives together. Our community is an ongoing experiment in the parish. We hope that good things will come of it, and I'm confident that one day we will find our way again. Some of us have been forgiving each other for ten years or so trying to live into Christ's strength and imagination for one another.

Chapter 7

Being Real with Our Pain: Holding Our Scared Wounds Together

Leaving Anger and Bitterness: Imagination in the Midst of Deconstruction

My own struggle with anger and bitterness over the last two decades has been horrifying and painful to say the least. This is a subject that goes deep within my very being. I don't often understand what is happening, but God has been kind to me. As the Downtown Neighborhood Fellowship has gone through many struggles and changes over the last decade, it has at times torn me apart and left me angry and bitter. So much potential has been before us and yet so much disappointment has ripped at our souls. I have had to live into the question: How do I protect myself from not getting caught up in all this anger and bitterness that is constantly so close to overtaking me? So many people who once loved us have abandoned us for an illusion of something better.

I fall apart at the thought of so much fragmentation and disillusionment among my friends who struggle to see beyond the reality of North American Christianity. Many people have a hard time understanding the possibility of a communal imagination in the midst of a Christianity that they have been taught which fosters dualities and religiosity. There is a great call of grace on our lives to become reformers in the midst of such tragedy. These distortions of our faith can be healed. We can be a part of that healing if we do not become disengaged due to all the anger and bitterness we might feel. We need not give up like so many have in the past. There is hope for a spirituality that is holistic and beautiful. There is a path to sanity.

About ten years ago when our Downtown Neighborhood Fellowship was making a transition to become a local expression, we formed an internship involving about twelve people. I had great hopes that this year-long internship would be transformative for all who participated. But it didn't exactly work out that way. It got difficult for me, and there were times that I would take it out on others. Dealing with the conviction that this internship was the best thing I had ever been involved in and yet stuck in the reality that others did not approach it this way was hard to take.

It may have been unwise of me to be expecting so much given the very experimental approach we were trying to embody. This was unfamiliar to a lot of us. This is not how we were taught growing up. Most of the others in the group had a hard time letting go of traditional forms of Christianity, but I had always struggled to embrace the status quo. Often when we would all meet together to learn and discuss, I would not say much. I would disengage out of fear and frustration. I wanted to make everyone more enthusiastic about learning and growing, but I felt as helpless as a little child. Whenever I spoke up it was usually out of fear, so the words I shared did not come out very gracefully. I would often try to shock others with very bold, controversial, unpopular topics and themes. This usually did not work as most of the people would write me off as strange or just kind of angry.

I wanted things to go well and for us to connect more as a community of faith over the years to come, but this too did not really work out that well. During the course of the year, I quit my job and moved into the neighborhood of Downtown Tacoma. Not many others did the same and this left me feeling frustrated. What I did not realize is that my frustrations and attempts to control the situation actually pushed me further away from others in relationship. This made it harder for us to develop some sense of community. I became not much of a friend to others and I started to live in resentment. My expectations had led me to a place of despair. What I thought could have been a wonderful integration of life in the neighborhood turned out to be nothing more than a bunch of people arguing and pushing back. This pushback continued the whole year and by the end of the year I had almost tuned out emotionally.

Toward the end of the internship, I became very angry and frustrated at the apathy that I had perceived among the participants. I was trying to control the internship by doing things that pushed people to participate in the internship with more life and creativity. I would force a conversation in social settings. I would try to shock others with my words. Sometimes I would avoid certain people just to show them how disappointed I was. I wanted them to notice my sacrifice for this internship. Wanting to feel appreciated and valued is what moved me to do all of this. But this just pushed others away from me.

I lost a sense of love for the people in my life at that time. Being so preoccupied with the success of this internship, I was not very empathetic or compassionate towards anyone. I was quiet at times, but I think others could see through me. Sometimes they tended to avoid me. I quickly turned into the frustrated guy in the group. I made everyone else feel uneasy and uncertain around me. So when I wasn't speaking out of my shock-value tactics, I was slowly disengaging as a way to control what was happening. Maybe I thought I could control the internship if I lived into these techniques to get people to do what I wanted them to do. This was not a very relational approach and I failed miserably in all kinds of ways which made me angry instead.

My motives were to help people to "see" and respond in a way that I perceived was following Christ. This is what I knew and understood at the time. I think I did a lot of damage to my own life by becoming so obsessed with control and the success of the internship. Taking this much too seriously was making it hard for me to have any compassion. This has been one of the hardest lessons of my life: to not be addicted to controlling the outcomes of the things I care about. I think this approach always damages relationships. It is hard to build some social capital with the people you are trying to control. I realized that this internship was causing me to become a Pharisee, a religious person who has forgotten love and cannot see God's movement in life. This is not what I wanted to become.

After all of this, most of the people in the internship lost all interest in our Downtown Neighborhood Fellowship. It was hard for them to move into the neighborhood and be at peace with it. So most of them never did. I was sad about this for a long time and looking back, I still feel moments of frustration. Things could have been so different. What would have happened if I inspired my friends with grace and joy as opposed to anger, bitterness, withdrawal, and frustration? If I could go back and do it all over, I would have invested more in grace towards others.

"See to it that no one misses the grace of God and that no bitter root grows up to cause trouble and defile many" (Hebrews 12:15). This bitter root will destroy our relationships and keep us apart from one another in everyday life. Bitterness and anger cause major dysfunction within us. But the communal imagination does not know bitterness and anger. It hopes for something better for our relationships. Bitterness and anger will murder the root of holistic spirituality that God is leading us to. When we live into bitterness and anger, we will not be engaged in the parish for long. The body of Christ will cease to become an expression of grace and will turn into an expression of wrath, anger, and manipulation. How tragic and sad. This is not what people need. We need to become an expression of grace to one another. Parker J. Palmer in wonderful book *Healing The Heart Of Democracy* writes:

> If you hold your knowledge of self and world wholeheartedly, your heart will at times get broken by loss, failure, defeat, betrayal, or

death. What happens next in you and the world around you depends on how your heart breaks. If it breaks apart into a thousand pieces, the result may be anger, depression, and disengagement. If it breaks open into greater capacity to hold the complexities and contradictions of human experience, the result may be new life.[1]

We will become broken. No question about it. This is part of life. If we break apart, we will find bitterness and anger. If we break open, we will become expressions of grace, compassion and love. This is the kind of life that one who has been broken open will manifest to others in the parish. The pain and destruction we do to our lives when we choose to be broken apart is frightening. We destroy our humanity in the process.

"Get rid of all bitterness, rage and anger" (Ephesians 4:31). Bitterness and anger will not nurture us as the body of Christ. They will destroy all the potential that we could attain together. Becoming an expression of grace is full of unlimited possibilities that we cannot even fathom. Grace overcomes bitterness and anger. God is not bitter or angry, but is instead full of grace, love and beauty. We need to have a communal imagination to become an expression of God's grace in this life. The communal imagination will heal us from the dangers of bitterness and anger. So many things happen in life that can break us apart, but we need to refuse to allow that to happen. Christ will lead us on the path of grace. He will break us open again and again. He will lead us to become the expression of grace that he has taught us to be as the body of Christ in the parish.

"But now you must rid yourselves of all such things: anger, rage" (Colossians 3:8). Anger cannot be a part of who we are as the body of Christ. It must not take over within us. Jesus teaches of the dangers of harboring anger towards others. "You have heard that it was said to the people long ago, 'Do not murder, and anyone who murders will be subject to judgment. But I tell you that anyone who is angry with his brother will be subject to judgment'" (Matthew 5:21-22). We

---

[1] Palmer, *Healing the Heart of Democracy*, 18.

become subject to judgment and lose sight of grace when we become angry and bitter. We must not get trapped in this deceptive way of being. Jesus is saying to us that staying angry is equal to committing murder. Grace is buried when we hold on tightly to anger.

We must let go of all anger and bitterness or they will destroy the communal imagination. It is worth quoting Dietrich Bonhoeffer at length here:

> Anger is always an attack on the brother's life, for it refuses to let him live and aims at his destruction. Jesus will not accept the common distinction between righteous indignation and unjustifiable anger. The disciple must be entirely innocent of anger, because anger is an offence against both God and his neighbor. Every idle word which we think so little of betrays our lack of respect for our neighbor, and shows that we place ourselves on a pinnacle above him and value our own lives higher than his. The angry word is a blow struck at our brother, a stab at his heart: it seeks to hit, to hurt and to destroy. A deliberate insult is even worse, for we are then openly disgracing our brother in the eyes of the world, and causing others to despise him. With our hearts burning with hatred, we seek to annihilate his moral and material existence. We are passing judgment on him, and that is murder ...[2]

When we are angry, we cannot live into the gospel and become expressions of God's grace as the body of Christ together in the parish. Our everyday lives will be wasted without grace for one another. "... for man's anger does not bring about the righteous life that God desires" (James 1:20). New Monastics Shane Claiborne and Jonathan Wilson-Hartgrove put it this way:

> ... if you get involved with God's people, you will get hurt. The Holy Spirit makes it possible—compels us, even—to share lives with one another, live together, do each other's dirty work, offer hospitality, make peace, share money, raise kids together, start co-opts and serve our neighbors. But if you do all those things with

---

[2] Bonhoeffer, *The Cost of Discipleship*, 127-128.

broken people (and broken people are the only kind available), you will hurt each other. You will be betrayed in one way or another.[3]

These are tough words from two practitioners who know the cost of the communal imagination. We will become wounded and hurt in the process of being in relationship with others in our neighborhood. The body of Christ will wound us as we share life together in the parish. Reacting to our wounds in anger is not walking in the Spirit. Responding in grace is. God's grace is so much bigger than all our wounds. Christ showed immeasurable grace despite facing crucifixion. We have wounded and hurt Jesus over and over again in our lives and he always shows grace. We need to imitate his ways and show grace to one another as the body of Christ in everyday life. Our anger and bitterness can't have the final say. Grace must face our anger and overcome it.

If we can imbue our wounds with the sacred, we will cultivate the communal imagination. We will become sustainable in all we do relationally. We will see relational revelations all around us in everyday life. If there is no sense of the sacred in our wounded state, we will soon become so angry and bitter that grace will not be found. Without grace, we will carry around in our veins nothing but poison. We will die a miserable death in isolation thanks to our tight grip on anger and bitterness. We have to find a way to embrace our wounds as something sacred and learn to express something beautiful through grace each time despite our hurts.

It is an ordinary miracle of everyday life when we embrace the sacredness of our wounds together in the parish. Franciscan Richard Rohr, founder of the Center for Action and Contemplation, writes, "If we cannot find a way to make our wounds into sacred wounds, we invariably become negative or bitter."[4]

---

[3] Claiborne and Wilson-Hartgrove, *Becoming the Answer to Our Prayers*, 69.

[4] Rohr, *Things Hidden*, 25.

"The grace of the Lord Jesus be with you" (1 Corinthians 16:23). Paul wanted the grace of Christ to be expressed among the believers in Corinth. He desired that the wounds they had inflicted upon one another would be overcome with a sacredness that would in turn cause them to be broken open for one another. The communal imagination calls out to us in our wounded state. We will be wounded, but isn't it better to live out of grace rather than anger and bitterness? Anger and bitterness are the easy way out. Grace expressed is the ordinary miracle that can sustain and nurture our relationships despite our wounds. If grace is absent, we will soon destroy one another.

Pain as a Medium of Reconciliation: Being Broken Open

When we go through sorrow and pain we can manifest Christ to one another through reconciliation and grace. Our biggest tragedies in life can be our greatest moments of reconciliation. Pain can become the medium that draws us together as the body of Christ in the parish. Pain and sorrow can keep us grounded in our presence one to another. We cannot run from our pain. We cannot escape it. Some pain is a part of every relationship. We will experience pain as the body of Christ. But our pain can become our teacher if we are open to it. Pain can bring us closer if our wounds, pain and sorrow are embraced as a sacred part of life that is necessary to our own human process. Pain can foster maturity and depth if we are broken open by it.

The body of Christ cannot afford to mask the pain of everyday life in the parish. We must become authentic with our pain. Jesus has not completed us. As much as we would like to believe it so, this is not the case. Our lives are filled with brokenness and pain. Most of the time we don't know how to show grace and love. But reconciliation can become a living, ordinary miracle among us. Christ longs to reconcile us together so that we can live at peace with one another. Macrina Wiederkehr, who has lived a monastic life for over forty years, says:

> We are absent from life far too much. Sorrow makes it impossible for us to be absent, and so, bless us with real presence. In the midst

of sorrows, distractions fall away, and we are there, raw and open, often confused, always vulnerable, little and great. In sorrow we are nudged to our depths. I do not claim to understand the mystery of suffering, but I often meet people who have walked through great sorrow; they seem to wear the face of God. These are the people at whose feet I yearn to sit.[5]

Sometimes I think that my pain is too great and there is no hope for reconciliation with others. But God constantly proves me wrong revealing to me how I can live differently with others in peace and grace. This is a countercultural posture that could bring great and permanent healing to our relationships. Isn't the cross all about reconciliation in the midst of Christ's deep pain?

We can connect through our pain if we are broken open to offer some grace to others. This gift can unleash relational revelations. Christ will be manifested among us through this posture towards life. Grace-filled reconciliation is one of the most powerful things we can practice. The body of Christ needs to live into this in our everyday relationships in the parish. Keri Wyatt Kent writes, "Compassion is a gift we give others and that comes back to us ... We learn that we are not alone, that pain can be what connects, rather than isolates, us."[6]

We need to give absolute attention to our pain so that it can teach us about what we do not yet understand about God, ourselves, and others. Pain will push us into a reconciling reality with others if we become broken open through a grace that connects us instead of anger and bitterness pushing us apart. Pain should not be ignored. The body of Christ will feel its pain in the parish. But this ought to be the medium for reconciliation among us. Pain teaches us what we cannot understand without it. Pain is human. Pain is sacred. Pain is divine. Pain is the initiator of a new imagination. Pain is full of possibility. Pain draws us into relational revelations. Pain holds beauty. Christ understands our pain. He was a man of sorrows whose pain led him to show grace

---

[5] Wiederkehr, *A Tree Full of Angels*, 36.

[6] Kent, *Listen*, 96.

towards us. Barbara Brown Taylor writes, "I can try to avoid pain. I can deny pain. I can numb it and I can fight it. Or I can decide to engage pain when it comes to me, giving it my full attention so that it can teach me what I need to know about the *Really Real*."[7]

After a few years into our transition into the parish, we had so much trouble that we almost did not survive. We were surprised by how hard it was for others to make the transition. We felt the cost and experienced a lot of pain. One day my friend Paul came to me and asked me if I wanted to continue on with him in the neighborhood. He said, "If you don't want to stand with me in this, then it's over. I need to take care of my wife." We were having such a hard time and had very little relational or financial support from others. We were on the verge of giving up on the Downtown Neighborhood Fellowship altogether and going our separate ways. We felt alone and defeated.

But as I thought about what Paul had asked me I just said, "I think we should keep going, and I will stand with you in whatever way I can." 'So we continued on. Almost a decade later, our pain has taught us so many things. It has taught us to live for the purpose of reconciliation both with one another and with all our neighbors. It drew out of us a passion for a new paradigm in our parish. It helped us to engage in relationship without objectifying others. Pain helped us to love one another. It has broken us open to become an expression of grace.

"Consider it pure joy, my brothers, whenever you face trials of many kinds, because you know that the testing of your faith develops perseverance. Perseverance must finish its work so that you may be mature and complete, not lacking anything" (James 1:2-3). There is pain in perseverance. But persevering in showing grace to others will constantly break us open to one another. The communal imagination does not close its eyes to perseverance and pain. The communal imagination knows pain. The communal imagination embraces its pain as a sacred wound that brings about reconciliation. Pain is the medium

---

[7] Taylor, *An Altar in the World*, 157.

that has the power to heal us and teach us reconciliation through grace. What a miracle that would be!

Our pain has a mysterious sacredness to it. Our pain calls us out in the sleepless night to something deeper. Our pain calls us to search for God within us. Our pain is something we feel, but do not see. This seems strange to our rational minds because it is mystical and beyond comprehending. We must simply live into it and trust the process. The glory of God is shown through our pain. Through our struggles in life, God is always present. Our pain reveals the present reality of God to us, through each other, here in this life we live. God dwells amid the pain. By his grace, we can start to become a healing presence and start to see God's glory all around us. Our pain is calling us to a beautiful reconciliation with one another in all dimensions of life.

> Therefore, since we have been justified through faith, we have peace with God through our Lord Jesus Christ, through whom we have gained access by faith into this grace in which we now stand. And we rejoice in the hope of the glory of God. Not only so, but we also rejoice in our sufferings, because we know that suffering produces perseverance; perseverance, character; and character, hope. And hope does not disappoint us, because God has poured out his love into our hearts by the Holy Spirit, whom he has given us (Romans 5:1-5).

It is through our pain that we learn perseverance, character and grace. This process will break us apart if we are not careful. It takes the utmost courage to face our pain in the midst of everyday life. The communal imagination faces pain. A Christianity that ignores pain is the most tragic of fantasies. It is fake, irrelevant and not human. "It seems to me," Richard Rohr notes, "that a Christian is a person who has the freedom to feel the pain that's part of being human."[8]

Our Downtown Neighborhood Fellowship has experienced so much pain over the years. For some people, it has been too much. They

---

[8] Rohr, *Simplicity*, 147.

couldn't take it and lost interest in our vision. For those of us who have persevered, it has been a dramatic shaping process. Our neighborhood has taught us of pain, reconciliation, grace, and glory. We have seen Christ living in each and every person. There is so much glory to be revealed through one another. We learn from the pain of our relationships in the parish together. It is ugly and yet beautiful and full of glory. We anticipate greater relational revelations of grace and reconciliation in the days to come. The longer we are here, the more that pain and glory are revealed through our lives together.

Downtown Tacoma has become a source of both great pain and deep growth for us. Our living here is out of our control. We just want to be a faithful presence of grace and reconciliation. Cistercian monastic writer Michael Casey says, "The effects of suffering are not limited to its immediate consequences. It has impact on life as a whole. Sometimes one needs it in order to grow more tender. As we reap our own harvest of grief, it is hard not to learn compassion. Our love for others is purified: the pain we have experienced makes us less and less willing to hurt anyone else. We become more human."[9]

It is hard to be human if we do not experience and feel pain. It leads us to greater depths of compassion and grace toward others in our neighborhood. We need to be shaped by this posture towards life in the parish.

Empathy and Friendship: Seeking to Understand Over Being Understood

> Praise be to the God and Father of our Lord Jesus Christ, the Father of compassion and the God of all comfort, who comforts us in all our troubles, so that we can comfort those in any trouble with the comfort we ourselves have received from God. For just as the sufferings of Christ flow over into our lives, so also through Christ our comfort overflows (2 Corinthians 1:3-4).

---

[9] Casey, *Toward God*, 6.

We need to pursue a sense of empathy, understanding, comfort and friendship with others. This is the call of the communal imagination. Do we like each other? Do we want to know each other? Do we care about each other? Do we share any aspect of our lives together? These are the questions that the body of Christ must live into together in the parish. God has comforted us and so we should comfort others with our friendship and empathy. There is no greater gift we can give to someone. This stems from love and grace. Relational revelation all around us awaits to be discovered.

We need the communal imagination if we are to be friends with those who are seemingly "different" from us. We need to seek to understand others constantly. This is how the gift of friendship is cultivated within the parish. Our imaginations need to be alive if we are to be in relationship with each other. We will fall apart without imagination leading us on. Our lives are full of differences and we cannot run from our connection to one another.

The imagination is inspired by grace. Empathy and friendship are gifts that hold us together as being a part of the human race. The body of Christ needs some relational empathy and friendship to survive in our local context. We need this grace to show respect to others in all their diversity and uniqueness. Wendell Berry, a long-time advocate of local community in North America, says, "It is by imagination that we cross over the differences between ourselves and other beings and thus learn compassion, forbearance, mercy, forgiveness, sympathy, and love."[10]

Where there is equality and empathy, there is friendship. We treat our friends with respect. We value our friends. We show grace to our friends. We love our friends. We need to befriend others who are seemingly "different" from us. We need to pursue friendships with others who don't like us very much. The communal imagination has empathy for others. We need to have empathy together as the body of Christ in the parish. We need to have respect for those who don't want

---

[10] Berry, *Sex, Economy, Freedom and Community*, 143.

to be in relationship with us. Our call is to seek to understand others no matter how we are treated, with respect or disrespect. French philosopher Simone Weil writes, "There is no friendship where there is inequality."[11]

> Greater love has no one than this, that he lay down his life for his friends. You are my friends if you do what I command. I no longer call you servants, because a servant does not know his master's business. Instead, I have called you friends, for everything that I learned from my Father I have made known to you. You did not choose me, but I chose you and appointed you to go and bear fruit—fruit that will last (John 15:13-16).

Christ values friendship. That is how he characterizes his relationship with us. We are in friendship with Christ together in everyday life. And so we need to call others friends just as Christ has called us his friends. Our parish teaches us to be not just in friendship with Christ, but also to be in friendship with one another. In this, we are shown how important our relationships are to one another as we share life together.

My friend Danny constantly reveals himself to me in friendship. He lives about three blocks down the street from me. I have known Danny for about nine years now. He has shown me what empathy looks like. Danny likes to play music on his guitar and I love to listen to the songs he has written about his struggles and dreams. He is also a great visual artist and I love to look at his paintings and drawings. Inspiring me to be a better friend by his actions, Danny always encourages me in our friendship. Being an expression of love and grace is his posture towards our relationship. He has such a great capacity for empathy and friendship. I love getting together with him and sharing life together through some common work together, over a meal, contemplation, or just talking. He constantly demonstrates what it means to be my friend. We have had our bumps and we don't always see things the same, but we demonstrate a friendship to one another that is manifesting Christ

---

[11] Weil, *Waiting for God*, 134.

to each of us. I see so much of Christ through my relationship with Danny and I am grateful to God that he is my neighbor and friend.

Another friend of mine is Paul. Paul loves to read and invoke brilliant conversations about complex things that I don't always understand. He loves me and has shown lots of empathy when I get frustrated in life. Paul lives several blocks down the street from me. He is very innovative and loves to talk about epistemology and locality. I think it is great and I love to be challenged to embrace new ideas. We eat together at times or study together or go for walks in our neighborhood. After a decade or so of knowing Paul, he has become a very good friend who has taught me a lot about an on-the-ground, practice-based theology.

I could go on and on about my friends in the neighborhood, but I will just mention one more for now. My other friend is Holly. I have known Holly for about ten years or so. She lives several more blocks down the street near Wright Park. We have done yoga together. We have gone running together at times. We have gotten together for coffee to chat. We have gotten together with our friends for dinners many times. We have watched movies. We have done crafts. We have cooked together. I constantly learn so much about empathetic friendship through her life.

There are so many people who have modeled friendship to me over the years I am grateful to have such wonderful friends who teach me what friendship means. Through our relational encounters over the years, I am beginning to understand that our common human life is connected through grace, love and empathy for one another. This is what we need to build the communal imagination. I always experience profound relational revelation when I am present to my neighbors in friendship.

We need friendships of empathy that will last years and years into the future of our life together. I cannot think of a more powerful witness to the gospel. The body of Christ needs deep relational ties of friendship, grace, and empathy within a local context. Esther Lightcap Meek says in her fascinating book *Loving To Know*, "Friendship is the consummation of knowing."[12] She goes on to say, "Friendship has the signature open-ended dynamism of the real."[13] Entering into friendship is how we connect to a holistic epistemology that does not damage us or our culture, but liberates our imaginations. Friendship holds relational revelations that we cannot understand any other way. It is so simple, yet we sometimes don't value friendship the way that we were created to. All of life is about friendship. All knowing comes through friendship. Friendship reveals to us how to live into truth. Truth, which expresses honesty, empathy and grace, is only revealed to us through each other. We learn what is real through friendship. It will be revealed if we do not run from those neighbors who are also our friends.

Friendship will last forever if we are empathetic to one another. Friendship has everything to do with our salvation and redemption, as the process of God's revelations are never-ending. We need to posture our lives in friendship towards one another with the least resistance to the real, so that we can touch something beautiful. Beautiful friendships reveal to us what is real about ourselves, life, God and the body of Christ. Friendship creates a holistic life in the parish. Our lives are integrated in the body of Christ, which is integrated in a deep communion with God, as well as with everyday life in the place we inhabit together. All are experienced as one. When this integration happens, we will become a subversive presence in many ways in our cultural context. And it all starts with an empathetic friendship toward one another.

Henri Nouwen writes, "Friendship is one of the most precious gifts of life."[14] Can we see the important role that friendship plays in our lives in the parish? Who are we without friendships? Friendships bring value and understanding to our lives. We are drawn into a relationship with God through our human friendships. The body of Christ needs to be a

---

[12] Meek, *Loving to Know*, 466.

[13] Ibid.

[14] Nouwen, *Reaching Out*, 46.

network of friendships in the place where we live. Only a network of friends can manifest God's love in its particular local context. The communal imagination is alive through friendship. Our human friendships reveal our spirituality via the on-the-ground experiences of real life. It all starts through always seeking to understand others over being understood ourselves. What a beautiful miracle this is when it is embodied in holistic ways in the parish.

Being Real with Our Pain

Chapter 8

Playing with the Spirit: Living Our Way into a New Way of Seeing

Seeing the Image of Humanity in Others: Bringing Dignity to Our Neighbors

At dawn he appeared again in the temple courts, where all the people gathered around him, and he sat down to teach them. The teachers of the law and the Pharisees brought in a woman caught in adultery. They made her stand before the group and said to Jesus, "Teacher, this woman was caught in the act of adultery. In the law of Moses commanded us to stone such women. Now what do you say?" They were using this question as a trap, in order to have a basis for accusing him.

But Jesus bent down and started to write on the ground with his finger. When they kept on questioning him, he straightened up and said to them, "If any of you is without sin, let him be the first to throw a stone at her." Again he stooped down and wrote on the ground.

At this, those who heard began to go away one at a time, the older ones first, until only Jesus was left with the woman still standing there. Jesus straightened up and asked her, "Woman, where are they? Has no one condemned you?"

"No one, sir," she said.

"Then neither do I condemn you," Jesus declared (John 8:2-11).

What an amazing story of how people can look at the same person and see something totally different. The Pharisees saw an adulterer. Jesus saw a woman. The Pharisees saw a sinner. Jesus saw a human person. The Pharisees approached her with judgment. Jesus approached her with grace. The Pharisees objectified her. Jesus honored her. Jesus must have already known this woman in his local context. He wanted her to feel her dignity and worth again in the midst of being disgraced by others. What was Jesus writing on the ground? Maybe it had to do with all the beautiful things about her humanity that those around her had forgotten. What a shame that people forget the beauty of each other's humanity. What a shame that the Pharisees could not see beyond the label "adulterer." They were blinded by their own prejudices.

At times our prejudices make it hard for us to see in others the image of our humanity. We see only what we want to see. The communal imagination longs to touch our humanity in the real contexts of everyday life. It is essential that we learn to see Christ in one another in the parish. Healing will come to us as we learn to see Christ in those around us. "Because we are learning to recognize the Christ in one another," Enuma Okoro points out, "we are also more susceptible to being healed just by being in one another's broken yet holy presence."[1] Sacredness lives in us because Christ lives in us. That means simply being in another's presence is to value that sacredness while embracing a holistic spirituality in the parish. The communal imagination looks for the image of humanity in others. Everyday life will reveal to us relational revelations when we see the image of humanity in others.

Christ was the ultimate image of humanity. He was a human being just like us. He breathed the same air. He walked the same earth. He inhabited a place that shaped who he was. He slept and ate and drank. He had relationships. He struggled with emotions. He laughed and

---

[1] Okoro, *Reluctant Pilgrim*, 148.

cried. We were all made in his image and that is reflected in our humanity.

Our lives call out to the indwelling Christ in each of us in everyday life. We do that through grace. We are drawn to tease out in one another this image of Christ. How do we do that? "Honor one another above yourselves" (Romans 12:10). Grace and honor will always lead to the communal imagination. When we honor others we will see the image of humanity that lies deep within them. Jesuit Mark E. Thibodeaux says in his book *Armchair Mystic*, "I am to call forth the Christ I see in others and to be a sort of mirror for others so that they may see the image of God that they are."[2]

When we see in each other the image of our humanity, there will be a spirit of reconciliation that constantly lives within us as we go about our everyday lives together in the parish. When we see the image of our humanity in each other, we will become better at relationships. We will become practicing, relational healers in the place we inhabit instead of destroyers of relationships. This is a miracle of grace. When the body of Christ awakens to this, there will be all kinds of relational revelations taking place in our neighborhood in everyday life. Debra K. Farrington writes, "The acceptance of others begins by recognizing that each of us is a beloved child of God. If we can see that in each other we may be able to better appreciate the differences between us. We may even grow to love the differences. At the very least, if we can see what is precious within each other, we can begin to offer compassion instead of criticism."[3]

"Here there is no Greek or Jew, circumcised or uncircumcised, barbarian, Scythian, slave or free, but Christ is all, and is in all" (Colossians 3:11). Christ's image lives in our humanity if we would have the imagination to see it. It doesn't matter who you are, it is there. We have been so programmed by an American agenda that it leaves

[2] Thibodeaux, *Armchair Mystic*, 167.

[3] Farrington, *Living Faith Day By Day*, 243.

almost no room for imagination. We constantly write others off as having little value to us because we deny their humanity and turn them into objects of indifference. This is damaging to the image of humanity that lives in each of us. On the contrary, our lives are to be an expression of grace together as the body of Christ in the parish.

One day I was walking down Tacoma Avenue in my neighborhood when a woman came up to me. She asked me if she could get a "sell." At first, I didn't know what she was referring to. Then I realized that she was a prostitute and was asking me if I would have sex with her for money. She came on really strong getting right up near me as I kept walking down the street. I told her no. I told her no again. Then she repeatedly kept asking me if she looked good. I told her she did, but I wasn't talking about her physical features. I was referring to her deep beauty, the image of her humanity that I was seeing in my imagination.

As she kept pressing me more, I wasn't sure what to do. A thought came to me: "Why don't you touch her hand and ask her what her name is?" So I looked directly into her eyes as I reached out my hand to introduce myself to her. I asked her what her name was. I practiced seeing this woman not as a prostitute or a drug addict or whatever else that would degrade her humanity, but as a human being with whom I shared many similarities as a fellow human being. As she stopped trying to sell herself and she told me her name, I could see a puzzled, somewhat surprised look in her eyes. Maybe she thought, "Why is this man looking at me without trying to use me or objectify me?"

She soon gave up on the sell and walked away, but I hope that she took away with her the image of her humanity that I saw in her in those moments. I have seen her around the neighborhood since then, but maybe she has trouble remembering me. She doesn't really respond to me if I greet her. She usually just ignores me. But I remember her name each time I see her. I practice remembering the image of humanity that lives within her.

I don't judge her because she prostitutes herself for money or uses drugs as an escape. There must have been a time when she was a young girl with big dreams. I often wonder, "What happened to her? What makes a person forget the image of their humanity?" I want to be friends with those who can't recognize the image of humanity within themselves anymore for whatever reason. I believe God spoke to me through this prostitute. My encounter with this women is hard to forget. I think about her often. God can speak through the most unlikely people, those we don't always see as "spiritual." Just like this prostitute.

Walker Percy says in his book *Signposts in a Strange Land*, "If I do conceive you as a something in the world rather than a co-celebrant of the world, I fall from the I-thou to the I-it. Yet I am not able to dispose of you as finally as I dispose of shoes and ships and sealing wax. There remains your stare, which may not be symbolized. If I am determined to dispose of you by formulation, I had better not look at you."[4]

When we fall into the I-it relationship we lose sight of the image of humanity in one another. We are all to be "co-celebrants of the world" as the body of Christ together in everyday life. If we can't do this, we shouldn't be in relationship with one another. We can't be in relationship with one another when we do this. There will be no relational revelations among us when this happens in the parish. The communal imagination restores the I-thou to our relationships where we can touch the image of our common humanity. We should do away with objectifying others.

We limit others when we try to suppress the image of humanity within them. Henri Nouwen, who gave up the academic life as a professor at Harvard University to live at L'Arche Daybreak as a friend to the physically disabled, writes, "Characterization is common but narrowing. Labeling is always limited. It reveals a lot about our own insecurities and gives us a false understanding of the real nature of our neighbors."[5]

---

[4] Percy, *Signposts in a Strange Land*, 137.

[5] Nouwen, *Spiritual Formation*, 11.

Labels keep us from knowing others in the fullness of their humanity. Characterization and labeling are anti-grace. They are cruel and mean, unkind and devaluing.

There needs to be a change that happens deep within us so we don't continue to create the same I-it relational context that is so prevalent in our culture. We need the communal imagination to see the image of our humanity and to be healers instead of destroyers of one another. Labeling and characterization will always harm our relationships in the parish. They block any relational revelations that could possibly happen between us. Ordinary miracles disappear. M. Robert Mulholland Jr. states:

> The boxes in which we try to imprison others are designed to assure that the other will be what we want them to be in our carefully constructed world. It keeps them at arm's length. It keeps them relatively safe. The box by which we control others enables us to accommodate them to our agendas. It also provides us some level of protection and defense against the threat they pose to our control of the world. Such boxes blind us to who the other truly is.[6]

Living by the Spirit: Embracing the Power of Honoring Relationship

We cannot live with a posture of grace toward others without walking in the Spirit. The Spirit honors all with respect and dignity and grace. The Spirit honors each human being in our lives. The Spirit is revealing the life of Jesus to us in the parish. The Spirit is about the relationships that we find ourselves in. Everything we do without grace and honor is done without the leading guidance of the Spirit. We ignore the Spirit when we objectify others. This grieves the Spirit because it slowly destroys all relational care among us. The body of Christ needs the communal imagination of the Spirit of grace. Jeff Imbach notes, "Spirituality is everyday life, lived in tune with the Spirit of God."[7] Our

---

[6] Mulholland Jr., *The Deeper Journey*, 124.

[7] Imbach, *The River Within*, 84-85.

spirituality has everything to do with our life together. Our spirituality cannot be separated from one another in everyday life.

The Spirit magnifies the relationships we have with one another in the parish. This is of the greatest importance to the Spirit. Without our participation in grace, the Spirit is limited among us. We sometimes struggle to see this in the place we inhabit, but it is true. The Spirit wants to bring reconciliation and grace into all our relationships. The Spirit leads toward a peace with one another. The Spirit works in very relational ways through us. The Spirit wants to partner with us in everyday life. Michael Frost and Alan Hirsch state, "In the organic, messy, often troubled, sometimes harmonious webs of relationship found among Jesus' followers you can see the richness and beauty and power of the fullness of Jesus."[8] Christ is revealed to us through the Spirit of grace in our relationships with one another. The Spirit is disruptive, uncontrollable, beautiful, subversive, relational, and powerful.

> But the Counselor, the Holy Spirit, whom the Father will send in my name, will teach you all things and will remind you of everything I have said to you. Peace I leave with you; my peace I give you. I do not give to you as the world gives. Do not let your hearts be troubled and do not be afraid (John 14:26-27).

The Spirit will teach us how to be in relationship with one another in a way that brings peace into the world. This has to do with honoring one another through grace. Through our grace for one another, we are living in the Spirit. The Spirit wants to tease out grace and peace in the place we inhabit. Our relationships will be characteristic of this when we walk in the Spirit. Our spirituality is about living in the Spirit. Christianity is a continual lesson in learning to live in holistic relationships of grace with others. One of my favorite mystic writers, Thomas Merton, says, "True Christianity is growth in the life of the Spirit, a deepening of the new life, a continuous rebirth, in which the exterior and superficial life of the ego-self is discarded like an old snake

---

[8] Frost and Hirsch, *ReJesus*, 169.

skin and the mysterious, invisible self of the Spirit becomes more present and more active."[9]

The longer I live in Downtown Tacoma, the more aware I am becoming of the subtle workings of the Spirit within me. The Spirit is drawing me to see others with grace and compassion. The Spirit is teaching me about reconciliation with others who seem very different from me. I have a friend in the neighborhood whom I have known for a long time. We have bumped up against each other many times on all kinds of things. We have disrespected each other through words and actions. We have disagreed and fought about things we feel strongly about. We have partnered in many ways together over the years, but there is this disconnection in our relationship that I'm not always sure what I should do about it. I love my friend, but we both find it hard at times to show grace towards one another. Over the last several years, the Spirit is teaching me to display more reconciliation, grace, and compassion towards him.

Recently, I have experienced a lot more connection with my friend on a relational level. The Spirit is healing us both and creating in us a more holistic relationship. We tend to get along a little better, and I am seeing that our disconnection has more to do with me than with him. I am learning to take more responsibility for our lack of connection and looking at how I can change instead of expecting my friend to change. I see this as an example of an ordinary, relational miracle among us in our neighborhood through the Spirit. The Spirit is constantly giving me many such revelations through my friend.

The Spirit is constantly nudging us towards more compassion and grace for others in everyday life. This is a hard practice to learn, but the Spirit is a wise teacher. We will learn to show grace and compassion in our relationships if we are walking in the Spirit. Our grace and compassion will heal us in many ways, but we will never know this unless we take action on those nudges. The Spirit is awakening us to this kind of action

---

[9] Merton, *An Invitation to the Contemplative Life*, 20.

in the parish. This is not a project that we do, but a posture that we adopt towards one another as we honor each relationship. Spiritual director Jan Johnson says, "Many of us lament that we don't have deeper feelings of compassion for people, but what is important is to be learning to respond to each nudge of compassion from God with merciful action. Our goal is to become continually more alert to these prods to action from God rather than waiting until we have certain feelings about people."[10]

Our humanity is honored when we become expressions of grace and compassion toward others in the parish. The Spirit is working within us to help us become this kind of expression in our everyday lives. There is nothing more beautiful than a life given over to expressions of grace and compassion in concrete, on-the-ground relationships. Our world takes notice one neighborhood at a time. "Those who live in accordance with the Spirit have their minds set on what the Spirit desires" (Romans 8:5). The communal imagination has a mind for the things of the Spirit. As we have seen, the mind of the Spirit is set on the local place we inhabit together. This is where relationships happen. This is where grace and compassion happen in everyday life. This is where relational revelations and ordinary miracles happen among us. James Finley, a former Trappist monk who studied under Thomas Merton, writes, "You begin to appreciate that every time you compassionately engage with another person, your reason for being on this world is honored and expressed."[11]

"So I say, live by the Spirit" (Galatians 5:16). The Spirit lives in the parish. The Spirit is inspiring our imaginations within us. The body of Christ must awaken to this life of grace that inhabits the local through the Spirit. The communal imagination is always led by the Spirit. David G. Benner, a psychologist and personal transformation coach, says, "Learning to become aware of the presence of the Spirit lies right at the heart of growth in Christian Spirituality. Apart from the Spirit

---

[10] Johnson, *Invitation to the Jesus Life*, 89.

[11] Finely, *Christian Meditation*, 285.

there is no genuine Christian spiritual growth."[12] The Spirit is teaching us to be in relationship with our neighbors. "Since we live by the Spirit, let us keep in step with the Spirit" (Galatians 5:25). The communal imagination always keeps in step with the Spirit in the place we find ourselves in.

My friend Danny has been living in the Spirit of honoring relationships for many years. When Danny first moved into Downtown Tacoma, he was shy and afraid of people, especially the homeless. He thought they were all dangerous. Danny was raised in a Christian home in the suburbs of Bonney Lake which is about a half-hour drive just outside of Tacoma. He initially thought that the city of Tacoma was scary and dirty. But as he moved into Downtown Tacoma after getting married to his wife Nichole, he started to learn from the writings of Australian missiologist Michael Frost. His books *Exiles* and *The Shaping of Things to Come* had a great impact on the way Danny started to experience his spirituality in everyday life. This learning developed into a practice that helped Danny stop being so afraid of others and start to embrace an incarnational way of honoring his relationships as he was guided by the Spirit. So he started to build relationships with his neighbors in the hope that he could develop some trust by the way he treated them in everyday life. He did not want to convert, fix, or give anyone some preconceived "answers to life." All he wanted to do was to listen, show grace, love, and become friends with others. Danny wanted to walk in the Spirit and honor the relationships that God has placed in his life in Downtown Tacoma. As a result, for the past eight years or so, all of this has been happening, God has been working relational miracles in ordinary everyday life through Danny's grace and love to his neighbors.

The biggest thing that has happened to Danny is that he has been profoundly shaped by it all. God has given Danny an extremely graceful way about him. Danny has become a powerful witness of an embodied way of love, kindness, and grace to his neighbors. It is a way of being

---

[12] Benner, *Sacred Companions*, 54.

that Danny has developed and practices in everyday life. He has learned to live out his faith through grace and, when necessary, with words. Being consistent and showing up in everyday life as he runs into a lot of the same people all of the time has been important for Danny in his journey of faith in the parish. His desire is to become an expression of God's beauty and grace as he honors his relationships and doesn't take them for granted.

Danny has learned to value the voices of others who do not necessarily identify with church, Christianity, spirituality or religion. He has seen the need to listen to them and honor their perspectives on life. This is crucial to his growth and understanding of how God is working in our culture today. These relationships have been teaching Danny so much about himself as he has learned to honor them as sacred. Fear no longer controls Danny's way of life as he relates to others in the parish. He is free to see that God can speak through anyone at any time. In his former safe existence, Danny had boxed God in. Now he has let God out of the box and is experiencing a God who is always breaking through the walls we put up to try to contain him.

One thing that Danny has learned is that relationships can be hard at times, but we make them even more difficult if we do not see each other as human. Danny has practiced putting his own thoughts, opinions, and judgments aside, learning instead to really listen to others. This allows Danny to honor his relationships in the Spirit of grace. He is learning more and more not to project his own stuff on others but to just listen, show grace, and see others as created in God's image.

Playing with the Spirit

Part 4

Walking in Humility: Searching for Authenticity within Us

Chapter 9

The Vulnerability of Risk: Getting Out of Our Comfort Zones

Living into Risk: Creating Experiments in Locality

We need to learn how to risk our lives in the parish. Our everyday lives need to embrace the practice of living on the ground in humility towards one another. Nothing is scarier than the practice of humility, because in humility we lose all our techniques of control and escapism. We are pushed out of our comfort zones. Our relationships become fashioned by a new paradigm of valuing one another's humanity. We can no longer walk past someone without regard for their wellbeing. This calls us to a new and disturbing degree of risk that will shake us to the core of who we are. This calls for new experiments around local ways of living relationally. Risk is about stepping into the unknown and being shaped by what we experience there. It is more mysterious than anything we have ever known and shatters all our propositions of preconceived ideas. The communal imagination lives by this kind of risk. It takes humility to live into authentic risk as a way of life. Is this not the call of Christ in the gospels?

How does change take place within us? It takes place through relational practice in the parish. We are shaped through the ongoing practice of humility toward one another. We are shaped when we risk seeing the humanity in another. We are shaped when we honor and value our neighbor. We need the humility to risk just being in our humanity and having some empathy for others who seem different from us. We need to risk seeing the commonality in one another. We need the humility to risk opening our lives to others relationally and trusting one another.

Relationships don't work without the risk of humility. Our imaginations are inspired by the intuition and creativity that risk cultivates within us. We need to cultivate the imagination to live into relationships differently than those we have known in the past. Relationships are to be valued and not taken advantage of. Relationships need gratitude not contempt. Relationships need honor not objectification. To have a new imagination for relationships involves risk, and it takes a lot of humility to sustain them. Mark Scandrette notes, "If we want to change, we have to risk new ways of being and doing."[1]

> If you have any encouragement from being united with Christ, if any comfort from his love, if any fellowship with the Spirit, if any tenderness and compassion, then make my joy complete by being like-minded, having the same love, being one in spirit and purpose. Do nothing out of selfish ambition or vain conceit, but in humility consider others better than yourselves. Each of you should look not only to your own interests, but also the interests of others (Philippians 2:1-4).

This passage calls us to attempt a great risk, the risk of humility towards one another. It encourages us to abandon any selfish ambition in our lives together and draws us to consider the interests of others. What a radical shift. What would happen if we had the imagination to risk living this way as the body of Christ in the parish? Our everyday lives together would become rich with relational revelations and ordinary miracles. We would all be constantly changed by one another through our mutual humility and shaped from within by our mutual risk.

---

[1] Scandrettte, *Practicing the Way of Jesus*, 175.

If we want to learn how to live relationally within the communal imagination in humility, we must embrace a posture of risk and experimentation. This is the framework for all relational innovation in the parish. "Risk-ability is vital to learning and innovation," say Michael Frost and Alan Hirsch.[2] There can be no learning or innovation in our local context without the ability to risk well in humility. Humility is the relational innovation that we need to inhabit in our neighborhood together. Humility is the risk of bearing who we are to those around us. It is about opening ourselves up to being shaped by our relationships. If we are to pursue relational learning, we must be open to the risk of humility.

This is where the communal imagination thrives. We need to unlearn so many things that we have practiced for so many years that have left us disillusioned. We need to unlearn the practice of being in a relationship with others that is void of risk and humility.

I have had to risk seeing others in my neighborhood in a new way. Whether I perceive someone as believer/unbeliever, Native American/ African American, Mexican/Latino/Asian, rich/poor, gay/straight, introvert/extrovert, artist/businessman, mentally ill/mentally stable, addicted/self-controlled, single/married, drug addict/alcoholic, physically disabled/healthy, man/woman, I am learning to honor all people regardless of my preconceived perceptions. I am learning to risk being in humble relationship with others. I am allowing my imagination to embrace what is real even if not openly expressed and thus hard to identify. This is important when I embrace another without fully knowing what will happen to me as a step into an encounter that involves some risk. Diversity and commonality collide creating something beautiful that in turn cultivates the communal. This is mystical and destroys all our techniques to control others and escape our relational context in the parish.

---

2 Frost and Hirsch, *The Faith of Leap*, 48.

Here's a great example of risk-taking combined with experimentation. My friend Holly and others from a group called Downtown On The Go tired of seeing abandoned buildings in the neighborhood that served no useful purpose, they took on an amazing project in community engagement. For example, on the corner of S. 11th St. and Market, they painted portions of the exterior of a beautiful building that was just sitting empty. They painted different parts of the building, creating four sections: Seeing Downtown, Working Downtown, Going Downtown, and Living Downtown. Under each was a caption with open-ended response lines where local residents could write messages on the wall in chalk.

The first section, See Downtown, was painted with yellow writing on a turquoise background. Underneath the heading was a sentence that began *I'd Like To See Downtown* ... Passersby completed the rest of the sentence in chalk. They said they would like to see among other things more small shops, free parking, a skate park, more bike lanes, greater safety at night, and fewer empty buildings.

The second section, Working Downtown, had light blue writing against a turquoise background. Its heading read *Downtown Works Because* ... The responses included the beautiful views, and because we need it. The third section, Going Downtown, had yellow writing against a turquoise background. Its heading read *I Go Downtown Because* ... Some of the responses included the people, to give, it makes memories, I love it, and the farmers' market. The fourth section, Living Downtown, had pink writing against a turquoise background. Its heading read *I'd Live Downtown If* ... Some of the responses over time cited more crosswalks, and more roofs over sidewalks.

Between the four sections there were two art walls that were painted a bright yellowish green and pink. Painted records had been hung on them with all kinds of artists' images. Painted on one of the walls was Downtown On The GO in large blue letters. Some of the differently colored records had images of Dorothy Day, a biking cowboy with a calf in front of the bike, a ballet dancer, a woman with stars and birds coming from her hands, bicycles, dancers, umbrellas, flowers, dogs, and a light-rail car. The colors ranged from white, black, and red to light and dark blue. On the corner of the building was painted a robot figure.

This project was undertaken around the time of First Night, a New Year's Eve celebration involving a lot of local activity. The hope of Downtown On The Go was to get people thinking about and relating to Downtown Tacoma in new ways. They wanted to get others engaged in writing on the walls of this abandoned building to reflect on the assets of Downtown Tacoma, all its beauty and potential. Themes of community, local economy, built environment, pedestrian-friendly, neighborliness, beauty, safety, social capital, all came out of this local risk-taking experiment by Downtown On The GO! Hundreds of people came together to view, write on the walls, and engage in new ways of thinking about Downtown Tacoma thanks to this work of love for the neighborhood. It has inspired some relational movement in terms of caring for Downtown Tacoma and taking responsibility for it with love, humility, and deep joy.

In order to risk all that we are to follow Christ, we have to live in humility and risk being in relationship with others. There is no way of being in relationship with Christ without being in relationship with one another. The humility that is required to live this way is intense and needs to be constantly cultivated in our everyday lives together. The communal practice of humility and experimentation is sustained in us through taking small risks of relational vulnerability. This will require learning some new ways of imagining how to relate to one another in the parish.

It will be worth the pain and struggle because in the discovery of coming to know one another more we also come to know Christ more. Christ is constantly revealed to us through the place where we live, where we cannot control or escape our local context. In this we have to learn to be in relationship with one another in a way that fosters humility, risk and experimentation. Twentieth-century mystic Thomas

Merton states, "And sooner or later, if we follow Christ we have to risk everything in order to gain everything."[3]

We might think it is okay to live in a way that is safe, defended and protected from all that would disturb us. We have great allegiance to being comfortable at the expense of what is true, real, and beautiful. We have become addicted to our chosen comfort zones. But Christ is drawing us to risk living humbly with one another. It is not always a comfortable place to be, because we are stepping into the unknown. We are taking a risk. It will shake us awake. It will kick us hard and knock us down at times. We will cry and feel pain. But there is a mysterious goodness and sanity about it that is hard to explain. The fear that seizes us to hang on for dear life to the comfortable damages the communal imagination by stifling the potential of what could be.

A life that's safe is boring. We seek safety in nice houses, isolated mortgages, and important careers. Not that these things are bad in themselves, but having them can oftentimes rob us of our imaginations. They can confine us to a box in which we stay trapped for the rest of our lives. When we remove all risk and humility from our lives in the parish, we become boring and vicarious. We become blind to any alternative way to live. We give up on the communal imagination. And safe inside our comfort zones, we can become angry and unpleasant to be around.

It is a risk to move in step with a God who is living and alive in the place that we inhabit together. It is a risk to move and live with others where diversity and commonality collide in humility. It is sad to think that God is being ignored in our neighborhood. It takes risk to humbly enter into a new imagination with one another. We need the courage to let go of playing it safe all the time and seeing risk as an enemy. If we develop a hospitable relationship with risk, with discovery as our passion, we will start acting in humility, and we will coax the communal imagination to come out of hiding. Esther De Waal writes, "To follow a

---

[3] Merton, *Thoughts in Solitude*, 34.

God who moves and who expects us to move with him is a risky undertaking. It means not playing safe."[4]

Brokenness: The Authenticity of Life Together

Brokenness is the inner world within us all. We have to find the humility to live with our brokenness in ways that bring us together rather than pull us apart. Everyone has trouble living with their brokenness. The body of Christ needs to practice a way of life that demonstrates reconciliation and peace in our relationships in the parish. Christ taught his disciples to love one another in humility. Brokenness and humility are intertwined with our inner lives. Together, they bring a beautiful healing into our relationships. Jesus lived in brokenness and with humility. He demonstrated this all his life: from birth to death and so much in-between—as a carpenter's son, his interactions with people, serving others, being misunderstood by his family and his followers, the last supper, washing his disciples' feet, in the Garden of Gethsemane, his suffering for the sake of the world. Christopher L. Huertz, co-director of Word Made Flesh, says in his book *Simple Spirituality*, "Brokenness is thus the sign of Jesus. He takes us broken and blesses us with community; in that community we are broken again and given to the world as agents of healing and redemption."[5]

We are called to be this "sign of Jesus" in everyday life. Christ lives in us through our own brokenness, humility, and authenticity. This is the sign of his Spirit within us as the body of Christ in the place we inhabit together. Our brokenness could be our greatest strength when directed toward healing and reconciliation in the neighborhood. We cannot pretend that our pain and our brokenness are not real. We cannot pretend that we are fine and don't need anyone's help. Jesus leaves us in the pain of our brokenness. We struggle all our lives to understand the human experience.

---

[4] De Waal, *Lost in Wonder*, 87.

[5] Heuertz, *Simple Spirituality*, 130.

It is a constant process of lifelong discovery. We are discovering ourselves, one another, and God constantly if we are aware. We spend all our lives trying to discover meaning and purpose. We live into the questions, into the mystery, into the unknown. Sometimes we feel overwhelmed and we want to give up in disillusionment. It is too hard and requires too much pain and suffering. We can't seem to face our own brokenness with humility and authenticity. We strive to find our humanity and struggle our whole lives on the questions before us.

"Humility is necessary," writes Martin Laird, "if we are to see into our wounds."[6] Through humility we can start to understand our afflictions as something beautiful, as something sacred. They are shaping us into who we are becoming. We cannot see what we need to see in our wounds without humility, without brokenness. We cannot close our eyes to our wounds. It is important to embrace the pain of brokenness and just let it be.

It is okay to be broken. It is okay to feel pain. It is okay to be depressed sometimes. It is okay to feel discouraged. Christ experienced it all. The bloody wounds on Christ's body are something we can identify with in our brokenness and humility. The ultimate expression of Christ's brokenness and humility is revealed in his last supper with his disciples.

> And he took bread, gave thanks and broke it, and gave it to them, saying, "This is my body given for you; do this in remembrance of me."
>
> In the same way, after the supper he took the cup, saying, "This cup is the new covenant in my blood, which is poured out for you" (Luke 22:19-20).

In the midst of everyday life together, our Downtown Neighborhood Fellowship has created a meeting space where we can remember our brokenness by partaking in communion together. It is an intentionally shaped environment where we hope to remember our brokenness and

---

[6] Laird, *Into the Silent Land*, 126.

the brokenness of Christ through his body and blood given for us. We strive to remember the humility and brokenness of Jesus through bread and wine. It is so encouraging to remember that our lives are one with the life of Christ in our neighborhood.

We hope to be a faithful presence of relational care in the parish. We seek to learn how to live humbly with one another. We remember that we cannot escape our brokenness. We hope for a miracle in order to stay connected and have the strength to get along, facing one another in everyday life. We remember that the sign of Jesus is his brokenness. And we need to live into our brokenness with courage, authenticity, and humility. We say to each other, "This is Christ's body broken for you," as we pass the bread. We hope to remember his brokenness in all that we do and in every relationship. Alan E. Nelson writes in his book *Embracing Brokenness*, "Jesus was our example of brokenness. His birth incarnated the concept. He defiled common sense by coming as a baby, small, helpless, innocent, powerless, simple, poor, uneducated, and dependent."[7]

The birth, life and death of Jesus all demonstrate his brokenness in multiple ways. He was poor, unrecognizable, rejected, persecuted, suffered pain, came from the most unlikely of places. Christ's whole life was a demonstration of humility and brokenness. Most of us probably would not have recognized Jesus in his day if we saw him. He was too common and too broken to be recognized. Our preconceived perceptions sometimes want Christ to be something he is not. He most likely would not fit our picture of a good American. He was too weak for that. His brokenness and humility are unfamiliar to our Western forms of spirituality.

As we embrace humility and authenticity toward one another, we begin to grasp the communal imagination. Our imaginations become stirred with new ways to live out the gospel in our relationships with one another in the parish. We begin to discover life through our brokenness

---

[7] Nelson, *Embracing Brokenness*, 85.

together. We start helping others through the pain of living. We take on a humility that connects us relationally. June Ellis, who embraced a Quaker spirituality of authenticity says: "We are all wounded; we all feel inadequate and ashamed; we all struggle. But this is part of the human condition; it draws us together, helps us to find our connectedness."[8]

We all feel the pain of brokenness. If we don't, we are not being authentic. Life can be extremely difficult at times and we need to respond to life in humility toward one another. We need to be gentle in our brokenness. Christ lives through our brokenness so we need not fear it. Our lives should not be consumed with our brokenness, but should be lived in an authentic humility in everyday life. Our woundedness and brokenness are common to us all and everyone knows struggle. But these are the things that can bring us together if we allow humility to flourish and connect us instead of pull us away from one another.

To live into an authentic spirituality, we have to embrace our brokenness. Brokenness is so much a part of the human experience that we need to find a way to live with it as we share life with others in everyday life. To be whole is to embrace our common brokenness and our human pain together in the parish. It is to take on an authentic humanity that feels what is real in our bodies. It is facing what is hard about ourselves and one another. To experience brokenness is essential to life. To experience brokenness is essential to our authenticity as human beings. Christ calls us to feel our brokenness and to live through it. That requires some sense of humility. Life is messy and relationships can hurt. But we are asked to be faithful in humility toward one another at all costs, in all things. "Wholeness does not mean perfection: it means embracing brokenness," says influential writer Parker J. Palmer, "as an integral part of life."[9]

---

[8] Ellis, "Growing Together," 145.

[9] Palmer, *A Hidden Wholeness*, 5.

Showing Vulnerability: The Human Connecting Point

The body of Christ has to demonstrate vulnerability within our network of relationships in the parish. Without the humility of vulnerability, there will be very little authentic relationship between us. There will be very little human connection in everyday life. We usually don't like to share our pain, our brokenness, our struggles, our fears, our insecurities, our weaknesses, or our cluelessness. We do not like to admit that our perceptions of things might be wrong. We do not like to admit that we feel incomplete even though we have faith in God. We do not like to admit that we need to let go of trying to control life and that we have trust issues. We do not like to admit that sometimes we have no desire for God at all. We sometimes do not like to learn from or listen to others. There is a real problem in our relationships if we cannot live into a freedom that promotes vulnerability. The communal imagination needs vulnerability to be alive among us. Innovative local practitioner Mark Scandrette states so clearly, "The kind of belonging and transformation that is promised through practicing the way of Jesus requires us to be vulnerable with each other and to work through the difficulties that result from having our brokenness exposed."[10]

We are shaped through how we practice vulnerability with one another. The way of Jesus leads us there. We realize that we need one another more than we sometimes realize. Our weakness and brokenness become revealed through our relationships in the parish. Our spirituality becomes no longer a show of piety, but instead becomes a demonstration of humility through practicing vulnerability in everyday life.

Where there is vulnerability, there is humility. Where there is humility, the life of Christ is living within us. It can be hard to let ourselves be exposed for who we really are in all of our pain, but it is a practice that the body of Christ must take seriously if we want to be relational in the local context we inhabit. "Therefore I will boast all the more gladly

---

[10] Scandrette, *Practicing the Way of Jesus*, 161.

about my weaknesses, so that Christ's power may rest on me. That is why, for Christ's sake, I delight in weaknesses, in insults, in hardships, in persecutions, in difficulties. For when I am weak, then I am strong" (2 Corinthians 12:9-10).

When we demonstrate some humility and practice vulnerability with one another, that is when we are most fully walking in the Spirit of Christ. When we are weak and vulnerable, that is when we experience God's power within us. A theology of place can only be lived into through vulnerability. There is no colonialism with vulnerability because it will help us not to impose our way of life on anyone and lead us instead through living into our questions about the mystery of life. There is no colonialism with humility because it will lead us into deeper honesty around connecting with others through our struggles. There is no colonialism when we learn to listen and expose our own brokenness to others through our vulnerability. The place we inhabit will require that we be vulnerable if we want to stay there for any length of time. Our relationships will demand it if we seek to live in humility with one another.

Living in vulnerability is something my friend Holly has done quite well over the years. Vulnerability is to Holly being at a place where you can't hide. It is being with people in raw emotion without having to fix anything. For Holly, vulnerability creates a space that allows for darkness.

When Holly first moved into the neighborhood, our Downtown Neighborhood Fellowship was going through a major transition. She embraced a lot of questions being asked such as: Who are the people Christ loved and was closest to? What does accountability mean? What does a leader look like? What is our responsibility to the community? How important is our theology? What is the identity of the church? She had struggled through her own family's perceptions, and these questions rocked the foundations of the Christianity she had been raised on to the core. But by listening to her authentic inner voice, and living into the confusion these questions caused her, Holly has become a major part of our neighborhood.

Holly feels it is our pain that connects us through vulnerability. She has found that you can't always give to others at certain times in your life, and that you don't always have to be strong. Holly has been able to accept both sides of herself: her strengths and weaknesses, the responsibilities and limitations that make her who she is. She has discovered that our vulnerabilities are actually some of our greatest gifts to the world around us.

Vulnerability is so mysterious. It flies in the face of reason. It just doesn't make sense to live into vulnerability. Humility and vulnerability are both confusing to lives that are built upon escape and control. Yet vulnerability breaks through to what is real both in ourselves and our relationships. If we are to live our lives trusting in God, then we must understand the deep spirituality of vulnerability and humility. It unleashes relational revelations in the place we live. Through vulnerability we learn to live life as a process of discovery through our relationships in the parish. Franciscan Richard Rohr says, "Apparently God is actually vulnerable, and we discover both God and ourselves in the mystery of that vulnerability."[11]

I have a friend who has gone through a painful divorce. Sometimes she seems fine. But sometimes she breaks down and cries. Sharing the pain she experiences, and realizing her life will never be the same, makes her very vulnerable. Figuring out how God fits into all of this is difficult for her. I can see the pain in her eyes as her life unravels. At her age, she never thought that she would be divorced and single again. Now she is alone and wounded. Learning to go on with her broken life in vulnerability is not easy. But she has not isolated herself from others in the neighborhood and she is learning how to live with vulnerability and humility. Her vulnerability is a powerful demonstration of the gospel in our neighborhood. Struggling not to be bitter and resentful about what

---

[11] Rohr, *Everything Belongs*, 133.

has happened, she is embracing her new life with a willingness to become vulnerable. She could have shut herself down and disengaged from her local context, but instead she is living into life with a beautiful spirit. It is incredible to see what the power of God can do in our midst with one who embraces vulnerability.

We limit ourselves when we choose not to be vulnerable. We can only go so far in life without it. Vulnerability reveals the pain that connects us all as human and alive, while it stimulates the imagination to new heights. "Without vulnerability," Paul R. Decker writes, "the experience of God, life, and others will be very limited."[12] If all we want or think we need is a limited experience of God, then we disengage ourselves from any sort of vulnerability. The body of Christ needs to be vulnerable if it is to follow in the way of truth. There is no truth to our lives without vulnerability. There is no truth to our relationships without vulnerability. There is no truth to our relationship with God without vulnerability. Vulnerability needs to live deep within our faith in the parish. Without vulnerability we should not speak another word.

"St. Francis of Assisi," Paula Huston notes, "probably the most beloved saint who ever lived ... believed that this experience of complete vulnerability was the central message of the Gospels."[13] Many of us have been taught that certainty is a more powerful witness to the gospel than vulnerability, but St. Francis thought otherwise. Can you imagine what would happen to our relationships if we lived into an authentic and humble mutual vulnerability? It would revolutionize our relationships in everyday life together in all kinds of ways. It would cultivate the communal imagination.

Women are usually good at living into vulnerability in their relationships. But men are usually not so good at it. Men usually express less humility than women do. Women usually thrive on relationships of vulnerability. Men usually thrive on what they've accomplished than

---

[12] Dekar, *Community of the Transfiguration*, 99.

[13] Huston, *The Holy Way*, 186.

they do their relationships. Maybe God is calling us to a more feminine-type wisdom in the parish with vulnerability in our relationships being the central message. Isn't it interesting how the Book of Proverbs refers to wisdom in the feminine? "Does not wisdom call out? Does not understanding raise her voice? On the heights along the way, where the paths meet, she takes her stand" (Proverbs 8:1-2). We need to embrace a spirituality of vulnerability that has a more feminine-type wisdom underlying it.

Humility and vulnerability go hand in hand. Both are essential if we are to live into reconciling, peaceful relationships in the parish. We are always being pushed beyond ourselves when living into humility and vulnerability. Our relationships demand that humility and vulnerability be functional. We need them to get along in everyday life. They are healing to our relationships and bring reconciling power. Our friend Michael Frost, who has influenced our faith expression in Downtown Tacoma writes, "Humility is about earthiness, reality, a true appreciation of our connectedness."[14] The humility of vulnerability connects us in a real way. It makes us face what is real about ourselves, our relationships, and the place that we inhabit together.

---

[14] Frost, *Seeing God in the Ordinary*, 185.

The Vulnerability of Risk

Chapter 10

The Honesty of Powerlessness: Learning to Live within Our Limits and Responsibilities

Powerlessness: The Subversion of Colonialism

We hate powerlessness. We want to be powerful people, but the truth is that we all partake of the cup of our own powerlessness. Humility is manifested when we embrace our powerlessness in the parish. In fact, there is no clearer manifestation of humility. Our powerlessness is where relational revelations happen as we learn to humble ourselves before one another in everyday life. Powerlessness reveals to us that the control we try so hard to hold onto is just an illusion. We cannot control life, not even our lives. We cannot control others. We cannot control the local context we live in. Why do we hold onto control? Maybe we are too insecure to embrace our own powerlessness. Henri J.M. Nouwen writes:

> What keeps us from opening ourselves to the reality of the world? Could it be that we cannot accept our powerlessness and are only willing to see those wounds that we can heal? Could it be that we do not want to give up our illusion that we are masters over our world and, therefore, create our own Disneyland where we can make ourselves believe that all events of life are safely under control? Could it be that our blindness and deafness are signs of

our own resistance to acknowledging that we are not the Lord of the Universe? It is hard to allow these questions to go beyond the level of rhetoric and to really sense in our innermost self how much we resent our powerlessness.[1]

Our Downtown Neighborhood Fellowship embraced our powerlessness by letting go of the controlled meeting spaces we once occupied. We had to let go of the "ministry" technique of impressive use of language and attractional growth. We have suffered criticism for seemingly choosing to "destroy" what we once created. The truth is we embraced powerlessness when we stepped into a new and untried theology of place.

Within that powerlessness, we've discovered that we no longer have control over our embodied expression together and the network of relationships that develop through it. Our powerlessness has shown us everything is a gift. It is organic and destroys the illusion of control. Our neighborhood has showed us our powerlessness through the pain and difficulties we experience in everyday life together. We can no longer talk to one another in clichés and propositions. Our local context and our relationships demand of us so much more truth than that. We are learning to embody a relational truth that is authentic and honest. Our powerlessness moves us out of the status quo. We have learned to become friends with our powerlessness because it will not go away. It comes with the territory of a holistic, embodied counterculture. We cannot escape our powerlessness. So we must embrace it with humility.

We resist our powerlessness. We do not like to let our powerlessness, weakness, limitations, and confusion show. It is so much easier to be colonial by imposing our ways on others and pretending to have all the answers. What will others think of us if we embrace our powerlessness? We seem to have to prove our "spirituality" and impress others with it all of the time. The body of Christ is being called through the communal imagination to let all of this end and dissolve among us. We need to learn to embrace the parish in all that our powerlessness

---

[1] Nouwen, *Reaching Out*, 57.

implies. Powerlessness is actually our ultimate freedom, but we just can't see it yet. Only when we become broken and vulnerable can we start to understand the beauty of our powerlessness. It holds within it ordinary miracles in everyday life if we would just trust the process of following Christ into our local context. Carl Carretto says in his book *Letters From The Desert*, "For so many years, for too many years, I have fought against my powerlessness, my weakness. Often I have refused to admit it to myself, preferring to appear in public with a mask of self-assurance."[2]

When we are relationally connected to others in our local context, we have to enter those relationships with authentic humility. There is no control here. There is no objectification. There are no longer any utilitarian purposes for our relationships. When are we going to wake up to our powerlessness in everyday life? The communal imagination has such a powerlessness to it. We have to lose every attempt to control and live life with open, empty hands that embrace our wounds as sacred. We see all of life as sacred when seen through the lens of our powerlessness. It shatters our illusions about life and one another. We are truly most beautiful in our powerlessness. The "religious" power that flows from the institutional Church is often truly ugly, damaging, controlling, and fragmented. The powerlessness we are talking about here is a subversion of all institutional power of colonialism.

There is a paradox to our powerlessness that comes about through our communion with God in the place that we live. It is only through our powerlessness that we are free to embrace God's great and precious promises of divine power that helps us relationally. This divine power is manifested in our humility and powerlessness in the parish. We participate in the divine nature through our powerlessness. "His divine power has given us everything we need for life and godliness through our knowledge of him who called us by his own glory and goodness. Through these he has given us his very great and precious promises, so

---

[2] Carretto, *Letters from the Desert*, 134.

that through them you may participate in the divine nature" (2 Peter 1:3-4).

When we place ourselves in positions of powerlessness, such as losing a centralized position of institutional power by becoming an embodied expression in a local context, we demonstrate a power that is relationally appropriate. This is the only kind of power that is worth pursuing. It is the power of humility towards one another in everyday life. It is contextual to our everyday local context. It can only be received as a gift from God. It is the power of the communal imagination in the parish. It has nothing to do with an institution of centralized power, but is manifested in our relationships through presence, respect, honor, love, humility, and empathy. This divine power is a complete decentralization of worldly power. This power flows from our powerlessness and operates at a grassroots level where no centralized power exists. Benedictine Joan Chittister notes, "It may be those who are powerless by choice who can best demonstrate the power that comes from not having power."[3]

We lose sight of our powerlessness when we try to leverage the growth model of centralized power through meetings and worship services that create many "missional communities" throughout a city or many cities. This is colonial in so many ways, doing harm to our neighbors because the centralized power is not embodied in a local context. This form of power thinks it has the answers for all particular contexts without being faithfully present in that context. This kind of one-size-fits-all power disregards embodiment, listening, loving, and humility, the countercultural expression in one particular neighborhood. It is acontextual. It is too big and too abstract. It promotes the franchise model of growth by disregarding contextualization. It fragments the body of Christ, making it into something it was never intended to be. It is the worst form of illusion and needs to stop.

---

[3] Chittister, *Wisdom Distilled from the Daily*, 9.

Out of our struggle to find some collaboration and support in Downtown Tacoma, my friends Paul, Tim and Ben created a nonprofit organization called the Parish Collective. We began in the Seattle/ Tacoma area of the Pacific Northwest. Tim and Ben are graduates of the Seattle School of Theology and Psychology, and Paul is the founder of the Downtown Neighborhood Fellowship in Tacoma. Together they formed a partnership that would foster mutual support, encouragement, and stories to inspire a new paradigm. The Parish Collective is about helping others share life together by becoming rooted in particular neighborhoods and linked across cities.

This is important because if a community is just rooted in a neighborhood without being linked to other places, then it can become too insular. Insularity can become a trap that can actually destroy a community. We need to be connected to others outside of our own locality in order to learn from other contexts about things we may be blind to. Linking to other places is an authentic demonstration of powerlessness, because nobody has all the answers on relational connection in particular places. Every place is different and life is messy. But we can learn from others and live into our own creative expression as it is discerned relationally in our local context. This will cultivate our imaginations in ways that break through the norm to engaging culture in a way that is beautiful and not damaging. Dwight J. Friesen, who is a huge advocate of the Parish Collective, says, "The practice of embodying the gospel in local settings and linking to others will become even more important in the post-Christendom era."[4]

The Parish Collective has been in existence now for about six years and has initiated a movement of locality in the Pacific Northwest, the West Coast and into Canada. It is spreading to the rest of North America as well as internationally. We have many innovative local practitioners with whom we collaborate. We host an innovative conference called Inhabit based on practice, presence and place. Our friend, Michael Frost, posted on Facebook this past year that he feels it is the best

---

[4] Friesen, "Formation in the Post-Christendom Era," 203.

conference of its kind in North America. Many theologians believe that this is the direction the Church needs to go if we are to embody the gospel together and not do damage to our society.

The communal imagination takes on a powerlessness of humility and vulnerability in the place it inhabits. It listens to its place in holistic ways. It respects the value of the people who live there. Richard Rohr writes, "You have to leave the world where you have everything under control, where everybody likes you, and head into a world where you are poor and powerless. And there you'll be converted despite yourself."[5]

We have to find a way to create a different world that is free from our illusions of control. Control always pushes away humility and powerlessness. Control creates dysfunctional relationships among us. We need a great conversion, casting aside control and putting on powerlessness as a way of life together. Embracing powerlessness will continually shape us more than we could ever shape anyone or anything else in a particular context. We have to understand the importance of allowing ourselves to be shaped by our powerlessness through others in the parish. It is more about us being shaped than us trying to "change the world." We are the ones who need to be converted in order for us to be authentic, truthful human beings in everyday life together.

The most popular messengers of Christianity today do not talk much about weakness or powerlessness. And yet this is the good news of the gospel, to live truthfully into the reality of our weakness and powerlessness. It is to embrace a life of humility so that we can get along peacefully in everyday life together. Powerlessness is not about achievement and accomplishment in some "missional" task. Success doesn't matter to the powerless. It is about being in our relational, local context with the power that comes from our powerlessness which in turn is a gift from God. Everything becomes re-oriented when we acknowledge and embrace our powerlessness in the parish. The life of humility manifested in powerlessness always values others, seeking their

---

[5] Rohr, *Simplicity*, 113.

interests and honoring who they are. This is the holistic counterculture that we are being called into through the communal imagination. Jacques Ellul says in his book *The Subversion of Christianity*, "How truly intolerable, then, is a message, and even more so a life, that centers on weakness. Not sacrifice on behalf of a cause that one wants to bring to success, but in all truth love for nothing, faith for nothing, giving for nothing, service for nothing. Putting others above oneself. In all things seeking the interests of others."[6]

Honesty: Living Into the Truth of our Relationships

We need to become people of honesty toward one another in the parish. Honesty is a manifestation of truthfulness with one another. Honesty is authentic. Honesty is vulnerable. Honesty embraces powerlessness. Honesty is about learning to face one another. Honesty is hard. We can learn to have the humility to be honest with one another in our relationships. But we must have the willingness to live into truth with one another. Truth is honest. Truth is about authenticity. Truth is relational.

Honesty lives in truth and Christ was the most honest of human beings. He was the truth, meaning that he lived in complete honesty all of the time. He was honest with himself, with others, and with the Father. He embraced reality with complete honesty. "I am the way and the truth and the life" (John 14:6). If we are to be an expression of truth in our neighborhood, we have to become honest in everyday life. Being people of truth means we will not lie to ourselves or to one another. Following the truth means we will be authentic and honest with others.

Truth is more about how we live relationally in humility, authenticity, and honesty than it is about intellectually believing in propositional statements and theological creeds. The truthfulness of our relationships will manifest the gospel in our lives. Our relationships should manifest the truth more than what we say. The communal imagination is honest

---

[6] Ellul, *The Subversion of Christianity*, 166.

in life and faces it with truthfulness. There can be no more lying to one another because that will destroy our relationships. Can we be honest in our humility, our love, our compassion, our gentleness, our vulnerability, our powerlessness, our limitations, our failures, our struggles, our prejudices? Are we honest about really desiring to know Christ more through our everyday life with others who live in the parish? Do we really care about others or just ourselves? We must face these questions honestly if we are to be the body of Christ in everyday life. If we are less than honest we cannot know Christ through one another. It is a tragedy when we cannot be truthful and honest with one another. All relationships require honesty for any kind of sustainability.

"Do not lie to each other, since you have taken off your old self with its practices and have put on the new self, which is being renewed in knowledge in the image of its Creator" (Colossians 3:9-10). This means we have to be honest with one another and do away with the religious clichés that keep us from relating honestly with ourselves, one another and God. Let's learn to speak in normal everyday language that everyone understands, thus demonstrating some honesty, humility and authenticity in our relationships. "There is no truth towards Jesus without truth towards man. Untruthfulness destroys fellowship," Dietrich Bonhoeffer says, "but truth cuts false fellowship to pieces, and establishes genuine brotherhood. We cannot follow Christ unless we live in revealed truth before God and man."[7] Living into truth means living into honesty. There is no getting around this. We must be honest with one another in everyday life.

So much of what I have seen of Christianity over the years seems dishonest to me. I haven't been inspired by it and I want no part of it. I don't like the attractional church culture because it is not an honest reflection of the early church, but rather reflects more of a Western business model. It is all about growth, consumerism, and turning people into commodities at the expense of creating a counterculture. This I find extremely sad and depressing. It is the last thing I want to

---

[7] Bonhoeffer, *The Cost of Discipleship*, 139.

invest in, and I empathize with those who are turned off by Christianity as a result.

North American Christianity is very good at offering people an opiate so they can escape real life. They are fed all kinds of clichés which are anything but honest. The North American Church is arrogant. It thinks it has all the answers about life. It pretends that pain does not exist and that everything is okay. It avoids any conversation about everyday life together within the proximity of a local culture, yet all the while pretending to be "worshiping" and "praying." Outside their church buildings, these individuals have little to no life connection to those other individuals they just worshiped with.

This is anything but a demonstration of humility and honesty. We who are in this situation constantly lie to one another. We are encouraged to never question the status quo. After all, we are told that being a Christian is about being a "nice person" who does not rock the boat. Thomas Merton says, "The saint must see the truth as something to serve, not something to own and manipulate according to his own good pleasure."[8]

When we live into the truth we will not control or manipulate others out of dishonesty. We will learn to honor one another. We will do all we can to never intentionally lie to one another. We will live into truthfulness as a servant who uses honesty and humility to liberate others. This is the call of the saint. It is a call to honesty and humility in the parish. The communal imagination upholds honesty and does not use lies to manipulate others in any way.

The truth of our relationships is an aspect of life that cannot be ignored anymore. The honesty, truthfulness, and humility we show towards one another says a lot about who we are as the body of Christ in everyday life. We will be shown to be either true or false by the way we live with each other in everyday life. Can we get along in honesty and humility,

---

[8] Merton, *No Man is an Island*, 198.

or are we living out another narrative based on arrogance and dishonesty? That impresses no one. But who can argue with honesty and humility? Our friend Mark Scandrette says, "It is a great gift to be completely honest with others."[9]

There is an interesting story in our neighborhood about my friend Liz and a friend of hers who she has shared a lot of everyday life with over time. Liz met her friend at work as the retail manager of a local bakery/ coffee shop. Through working together for several years a special friendship has developed between the two. Liz has entered into an honest, authentic relationship with him. She does not hide her own vulnerability, confusion, insecurity, and fear. She doesn't come across like she has all the answers for his life, but is instead just trying to figure out life for herself.

Her friend has had many interactions with those of Christian faith who have seemed to have an agenda to convert him to Christianity. Liz's friendship has showed him something very different. She has developed a lot of trust with him by a lot of ongoing interactions at work and in everyday life outside of work. This has gone on for a number of years over time. He feels that he can just be himself around Liz. She is not trying to "fix" him in any way. Liz loves him just the way he is and desires that he would live into his authentic self. She wants to show him the love of God through her life and the truth of their relationship. Liz has no desire to convince him intellectually about Christianity. She knows it needs to be embodied in the honesty and truth of their relationship in everyday life. Liz feels it is through her love, grace and humility that he will experience her spirituality in an authentic, beautiful way.

The biggest thing about their relationship is that he knows that Liz is not trying to change him. He has been hurt in many ways in the name of Christianity, so Liz is very careful to be sensitive to where he is at in terms of his views. But because of the truth of their relationship, they

[9] Scandrette, *Soul Graffiti*, 54.

have developed a strong friendship and he has come to trust what Liz has to say on the important matters of life simply because of who she is.

It is such a gift from God to live in honesty with one another in genuine humility. It is so rare that it is an ordinary miracle whenever it is sustained among us for any amount of time. "Live in harmony with one another" (Romans 12:16). We live in harmony with one another when we do not hurt each other through our dishonesty, whether that be through our words or actions. Harmony is sustained through honesty and humility towards one another. When we have problems it is usually because honesty and humility have been misplaced for some reason.

This gift of honesty is not to be taken for granted. It is the core of our very survival and it is how trust is developed between us in the parish. When it is gone we don't have much left to hold onto and we end up hurting one another. Christopher L. Huertz writes, "When our pride gets in the way, the face of Jesus can be elusive when we expect him to mirror our version of Christianity rather than the kingdom reality he embodies."[10] Our pride, arrogance, and dishonesty shield us from the humility and honesty we need to live in harmony with one another in everyday life. When we are in that place we usually end up with a distorted Christianity where it is hard to see Christ and one another at all.

Humility and honesty are the hardest of virtues to come by. Usually, we have to lose everything to embrace them. It seems we would much rather hold onto our arrogance, pride and dishonesty than embrace what would bring us relational peace. Conversely, humility and honesty will bring about a deep relational peace if we practice them in the parish. "Alcoholics say that without humility and honesty," Richard Rohr notes, "nothing new happens. These virtues, humility and honesty, are the foundation of all spirituality, but they are hard won. Most of us

---

[10] Heuertz, *Simple Spirituality*, 34.

have to crawl our way back to them. Usually we don't go unless the pain of circumstances forces us."[11]

Humility and honesty are core to our spiritual development as the body of Christ in everyday life. They help us to get along in life, to have respect for one another. We need to embrace them by our own choosing before life crushes us and we are left limping and bleeding from the wounds of our own making

Learning from Others: The Responsibility of Agency

"Submit to one another out of reverence for Christ" (Ephesians 5:21). We need to submit to and learn from one another in the parish. We should honor both genders equally and take a posture of reverence and learning from both the women and the men in our lives. Oftentimes women are better practitioners of relational care in a local context than men are. So we must not make the mistake of saying we can only learn from men. We also need to take a posture of reverence and learning from both the elderly and the children among us. The women, men, and children in our lives all influence our response to life through the difficult and not-so-difficult moments of everyday life.

There is so much these relationships can teach us. We need to embrace a humility that learns from others. Learning from others cultivates our responsibility of agency, our ownership to take meaningful action, as human beings in the parish. Learning from others constantly cultivates the communal imagination. As Benedictine Joan Chittister says:

> Humility is simply a basic awareness of my relationship to the world and my connectedness to all its circumstances. It is the acceptance of relationships with others, not only for who they are but also for who I am. I do not interact with others to get something out of it; I make my way with all the others in my life

---

[11] Rohr, *Everything Belongs*, 48.

because each of them has something important to call out of me, to support in me, to bring to fruit a vision of God in my life.[12]

Without a humility that is constantly learning from the gifts of others, we are dysfunctional. There is so much that can be teased out of us as a result of our relationships in the parish. Our relationships become so much more important in shaping us when we hold them with a posture of learning. When we see our relationships through the lens of humility we begin to learn from one another in so many ways. Our relationships help us to learn about God. God is most clearly communicated to our senses in ways we can understand through one another. We will all be better off. When men, women and children learn to see themselves as created equally in God's image and start to learn from one another, we will live out a more holistic spirituality together.

We cannot embrace a humility in which we are continually learning from others without a listening spirit. There can be no learning from others without listening to one another. Listening is intertwined with learning. We have to really believe that we have much to learn from others with all our commonality and diversity. We need to approach others with this learning posture of discovery. God will always surprise us through our friends when we learn to see them as our teachers and listen to them attentively. "Humility is an essential part of listening," writes Hugh Feiss who has been a Benedictine for over thirty-five years. "Only someone who believes he has something to learn is an attentive listener."[13] Listening to the women, men and children in our local context will manifest some relational revelations that can be found in no other way. The communal imagination listens and learns from others.

There has been so much I have learned from my friend Nichole who I have known for quite some time now. She is very intelligent and has a passion for our neighborhood. Nichole owns the Nurture Healing

---

12 Chittister, *Wisdom Distilled from the Daily*, 65.

13 Feiss, *Essential Monastic Wisdom*, 90.

Center and works as a massage therapist collaborating with others throughout the neighborhood. She teaches me a lot about joy in the midst of pain. From her I have learned the value of cultivating some compassion, hospitality and gentleness within myself. This is something I need others to help me with on an ongoing basis. The example of her life teaches me the many ways of how to have love for others and to be a friend to someone. Nichole teaches me how to see others in all their commonality and diversity. She teaches me how to smile and have an imagination for hope. I love to see her smile and laugh as we are interacting with our neighborhood. She teaches me to have courage for the things in life that are hard for me to face. The imagination and creativity that resonate throughout her life constantly amaze me. She teaches me about connecting more holistically with my body. She teaches me to commune with God in different ways. Nichole teaches me to be kind and sensitive to the others in our neighborhood.

I have known Nichole for about ten years now and I have only just begun to discover the many dimensions of life within her. My friendship with Nichole has led me to a much more holistic spirituality. I could mention here many more friends in the neighborhood from whom I am constantly learning, but I will stop here for now. I am so grateful for all the relationships I have developed over the years with people who have become my teachers in many ways.

We come to understand our humanity more when we learn from the beauty of each person's gifts. Everyone has gifts to bring to our local context. Our very lives are such a gift that we must not take one another for granted and stop learning from one another. This is so foundational to a sustainable way of life together. Humility will keep us in a learning mode of relating to one another. Our whole lives could be spent learning from one another. This doesn't necessarily involve teaching one another from some book or the Scriptures, though that is possibly a part of it, but rather the relational learning that takes place as we discover each other in everyday life in all kinds of intuitive ways. The tacit dimension of relational knowing takes years to develop, so we must not take this lightly. We have to enter into a covenant of discovery and learning from one another to start to live into humility toward one another. To learn in this way is the responsibility of agency that we are called to as we live as authentic human beings on the earth. We all have a responsibility as persons in the parish to participate in this circle of learning. We need to have the communal imagination to see that when we learn from others it is as if we are learning from God.

We reveal the Scriptures and God's nature to one another through our relational care. We are expressions of the Scriptures in everyday life together. I learn about God through you and you learn about God through me. How amazing! Thomas a Kempis says, "If your heart is right, then every creature is a mirror of life to you and a book of holy learning, for there is no creature—no matter how tiny or how lowly— that does not reveal God's goodness."[14] We are living "books of holy learning" to one another in the parish. We, the body of Christ, are the ones who need to be changed through one another. Maybe our evangelism should be more focused on ourselves, not on others. We need a conversion of imagination where we live into the reality of learning, listening, and becoming a people of humility. What a beautiful way to live our lives together! We receive others as "mirrors of life" to us as we become constantly shaped through our relationships.

---

[14] Kempis, *The Imitation of Christ*, 52.

The Honesty of Powerlessness

Chapter 11

The Unselfishness of Gratitude: Becoming the Servant of All

The Gift of Gratitude: Breaking Down Relational Dysfunction

Gratitude is so important to the communal imagination. Without it our imaginations will become oppressed and die right before our eyes. We must give heed to the wisdom of gratitude in our everyday lives in the parish. Gratitude will be the strength that sustains us throughout our shared life together. To ignore the gift of gratitude is the very beginning of our demise as human beings. We were created to live into gratitude for and with one another. Humility is intertwined with gratitude. Without humility there can be no trace of gratitude among us. We are most open to reality when we practice a holistic form of gratitude together.

The Scriptures say, "… give thanks in all circumstances, for this is God's will for you in Christ Jesus" (1 Thessalonians 5:18). When we embrace gratitude, we live into the Spirit of ordinary miracles. Sometimes nothing seems more difficult and impossible than gratitude. Gratitude is a miracle waiting to happen, but often the things of life that cause deep pain within us push it away or bury it. Gratitude was embedded in the life of Christ despite the pain and suffering he endured throughout his life. We cannot grasp life with intention and meaning without cultivating the gift of gratitude. Gratitude is so mystical and real within the human spirit. The possibilities are endless as to the beauty we can discover within one another through our gratitude. Gratitude enhances our relational connection to one another in everyday life.

My friend Gary has had profound awakenings when it comes to the practice of gratitude within the parish. He ended up moving into the neighborhood several years ago and has been a blessing to our Downtown Neighborhood Fellowship. Since coming into our context out of a brokenness that had caused him to lose a lot of what he had previously based his life on, Gary has been finding a deep sense of gratitude within himself. He has been an encouragement to so many of us in Downtown Tacoma. His life is now an expression of gratitude and relational connection. Gary feels this is how he was meant to live. This revelation didn't come to him through his accomplishments, but through his humility and brokenness.

When Gary experienced hardship in his life, others rejected and judged him. It was a painful experience for him to have to live through and he almost didn't survive it. But the people of our Downtown Neighborhood Fellowship as well as the Tacoma Catholic Worker accepted Gary into their lives. He has been a good friend to many of us and we couldn't imagine life in the parish without Gary. He has adopted a posture of simplicity, presence, humility, love, and listening. This all stems out of his gratitude for the grace he has been shown by so many friends in the neighborhood.

Gary has learned that living in the parish fosters a relational accountability because we will see our neighbors over and over again in everyday life. This accountability is not in the form of a signed contract, but it's still a reality in the way we express respect, humility, love, and care for one another. Gary is learning to develop healthy boundaries and to use the holy word "No" more often. This is bringing about a greater depth to his humanity and leading to healthier relationships in his life.

The community has become a sounding board for his life where others can handle honestly the questions he has and the decisions he needs to make. The relational values of the parish are continually shaping him. He is moving away from fear and into compassion, love, and humility with a deeper gratitude. Gary is experiencing that he doesn't have to accomplish anything in order to belong, but rather that his belonging is based on his worth as a human being as we relate to him with love, grace and humility. "Everything is a gift" is a theme that Gary relies on. This is leading him to have a posture of receiving life rather than trying to make something happen all by himself.

Gratitude is not rational and most of the time it does not make sense to us. Gratitude is from the Spirit and lives within each one of us. We have to find a way to open up the communal imagination to the gratitude that lies buried within us beneath life's hardships and disappointments. Our gratitude has the potential to be just as real, influential and powerful as our pain. Pain does not have to control every aspect of who we are. God has given us a spirit of gratitude that has the power to free us from being constantly consumed by our pain.

Gratitude and pain co-exist within us to create something beautiful and mystical. We cannot know fully what will result until they collide in everyday life. A big part of our liberation rests in our ability to practice gratitude. This is God's will because it connects us relationally to one another in holistic ways as we share everyday life together. William A. Barry states, "Profound gratitude arises when I realize through God's grace that everything I have is gift."[1] Everything in life is a gift from God. Our relationships are a gift. The place that we inhabit is a gift. The life we live is a gift. Our understanding is a gift. Our gratitude comes alive when we live through this paradigm of seeing everything as gift.

I have gone through a major struggle to embrace the gratitude within me. I have fought against gratitude. I have not always allowed its reality

---

[1] Barry, *Letting God Come Close*, 176.

to come alive within me. Because of this, I have had seasons in my life where I have struggled with depression. Gratitude doesn't make sense to me when I'm in pain. How can I be grateful for what is causing me pain? Most of the time I cannot see through my pain, and so I slowly become blind to the subsidiary dimensions that are trying to communicate to me in all kinds of ways. I lose the perspective of seeing everything as a gift. If I fail to see everything as a gift and my wounds as sacred, I quickly fall apart. I need encouragement from Christ to integrate gratitude into my life.

This has been one of the most difficult things in my life for me to understand. Gratitude is healing for my body. Having lived relationally in my locality for many years now, I have discovered that practicing gratitude is essential if I am to sustain my relationship with others, with God, and with myself. Gratitude brings about a mystical sanity that helps us to walk in humility with one another.

We cannot afford to miss the moments in life when gratitude is called for. Integrating gratitude into my life is an ongoing lifelong process. And yet it is so essential to our humanity because it has an immense power to shape us from within. It is worth noting David Steindl-Rast's wisdom when he says:

> The interdependence of gratefulness is truly mutual. The receiver of the gift depends on the giver. Obviously so. But the circle of gratefulness is incomplete until the giver of the gift becomes the receiver: a receiver of thanks. When we give thanks, we give something greater than the gift we received, whatever it was. The greatest gift one can give is thanksgiving. In giving gifts, we give what we can spare, but in giving thanks we give ourselves. One who says "Thank You" to another really says, "We belong together." Giver and thanksgiver belong together. The bond that unites them frees them from alienation. Does our society suffer from so much alienation because we fail to cultivate gratefulness?[2]

---

[2] Steindl-Rast, *Gratefulness, The Heart of Prayer*, 17.

Mark Votava

Practicing the humility of gratitude in our local context will open up our imaginations to our connectedness and commonality. Seeing our friends as gifts from God and allowing relational revelations to surprise us constantly will open our imaginations to see one another anew. To say "Thank you" to one another is such a simple but profound practice of gratitude. Do we alienate ourselves from one another when we refuse to say "Thank you"? Our culture suffers from a lack of gratitude. We would rather push others away from us than show them some gratitude. Showing gratitude towards one another could bring about some healing to our broken society.

The communal imagination needs a spirit of gratitude. Henri Nouwen says, "Authentic Christian community nurtures the spirit of gratitude."[3]

Gratitude has an authenticity to it that will tease out all the beauty that life has to offer us. Gratitude nourishes our relationships and gives us a peaceful rest in the midst of the stress of life and the pain it can bring. Gratitude restores our life's balance, which helps us to be whole in the midst of our pain. Our pain will not destroy us if we embrace gratitude. What a miracle the practice of gratitude is among us. It is a precious gift that we should never take for granted. The humility it cultivates between us in the parish is amazing. The communal imagination embraces gratitude in everyday life. Thomas Merton writes, "To be grateful is to recognize the Love of God in everything He has given us—and He has given us everything. Every breath we draw is a gift of His love, every moment of existence is a grace, for it brings with it immense graces from Him. Gratitude therefore takes nothing for granted, is never unresponsive, is constantly awakening to new wonder."[4]

Gratitude consists of responsiveness, awakening, and wonder. When we see everything in life as a gift, this process of discovery never ends. Every breath we take and every moment of our life are all gifts from

[3] Nouwen, *Spiritual Formation*, 65.

[4] Merton, *Thoughts in Solitude*, 42.

God. The times we connect with each other in everyday life are gifts from God. The sacred moments that make up all of life are gifts from God. The Spirit is moving us to embrace a life of humility and gratitude. We will experience new awakenings and new depths of wonder as we live into gratitude. There is nothing else like it for bringing about peace in our lives.

Listening is intertwined with a spirit of gratitude. We cannot embrace life as a gift if we cannot listen to all the subsidiaries of life in and around us. We learn to notice things that would be unnoticeable when we practice gratitude together. Keri Wyatt Kent states, "Being grateful is a way of listening, a way of noticing God."[5] We begin to understand gratitude when we learn to listen to all the things that are otherwise so easy to miss in the parish. We begin to be contextual in terms of the relationships that we hold dear. We break out of the male-dominated achievement mode of spirituality and embrace a more holistic feminine-style wisdom that rests and listens. For a lot of people, this is a much too weak, powerless, vulnerable, honest way of spirituality. But the communal imagination lives within this kind of life together.

Serving Others: Stepping Into the Life of Collaboration

"But we have the mind of Christ" (1 Corinthians 2:16). What is the mind of Christ? It is manifested through becoming a servant to one another in everyday life in the place we inhabit together. The mind of Christ is about humility. The mind of Christ is about collaboration in life. The mind of Christ is about powerlessness. The mind of Christ is about listening. The mind of Christ is about empathy. The mind of Christ is relational. The mind of Christ is loving. The mind of Christ is kind. The mind of Christ is honest. The mind of Christ is creative.

We need the mind of Christ to live within us. The mind of Christ is not the North American way. The mind of Christ is not arrogant. The mind of Christ is not religious. The mind of Christ does not seek power. The

---

[5] Kent, *Listen*, 19.

mind of Christ works at a grassroots level. The mind of Christ is communal. The mind of Christ has imagination. The mind of Christ is gentle. The mind of Christ is a process of embodying and discovering all that is beautiful in life. Dorothy Day, who is regarded by some as one of the most influential Catholics in American history, states, "The greatest challenge of the day is: how to bring about a revolution of the heart, a revolution which has to start with each one of us? When we begin to take the lowest place, to wash the feet of others, to love our brothers with that burning love, that passion, which led to the Cross, then we can say, 'Now I have begun.'"[6]

Our challenge is to find a revolutionary spirit of humility and love within us that will carry over into all our relationships in the parish. We need this revolutionary servant spirit in all we do. The revolution starts with taking the place of least importance. It begins with embracing a humility where we become a servant of others, and we see life through the paradigm of servanthood and not as an individualistic North American.

> You know that the rulers of the Gentiles lord it over them, and their high officials exercise authority over them. Not so with you. Instead whoever wants to become great among you must be your servant, and whoever wants to be first must be your slave—just as the Son of Man did not come to be served, but to serve, and to give his life as a ransom for many (Matthew 20:25-28).

This is such a disturbing passage of Scripture. Either we do not understand what Christ is talking about or we do not want to, because of the implications and the risk such a command would require of us as the body of Christ. And yet this is an entirely different outlook on life that if followed, can change our priorities and place our relationships on higher ground. Our relationships become the central focus in our lives when we become the servant of all. Christ is teaching us through this Scripture that greatness comes only when we honor one another by

---

[6] Day, *Loaves and Fishes*, 215.

embracing a way of life where we humble ourselves by becoming a virtual slave to others.

Christ is not playing games with what he defines as greatness. He lays out that it doesn't matter if you are a man or a woman, greatness is about becoming a servant to others in the place where we live. Men have a little more trouble with this than woman. It seems funny to me that most of our leadership examples are men who usually miss the boat and who have all forgotten what it means to be great according to Christ's definition. Women seem to understand this form of greatness better than men do since it is more natural for them to perform acts of care, love, neighborliness, and collaboration.

My friend Molly is such a great example to me of what it means to embrace Christ-like greatness. Molly is such a loving, kind, gentle servant to all the people with whom she is in relationship in our neighborhood. She owns a local bakery/coffee shop a few blocks from where I live. Showing up at work very early in the morning and helping others prepare the bakery products for the day is for her a regular daily rhythm. Molly collaborates with many diverse people throughout the day. She exudes humility and kindness to all who come to her bakery. When things are chaotic, she rarely ever gets angry and frustrated. She treats her employees with great respect and honor. They all love Molly and they all appreciate who she is in their lives.

Molly has helped all of us in the neighborhood better understand the teachings of Christ on greatness and on becoming a servant to others. She incarnates what it means to demonstrate greatness in how we are to treat others in everyday life together. Molly is a great listener and is very empathetic. If you were to ask her why she does what she does, she would probably tell you that it's no big deal. But in fact her ability to care for and serve others relationally is profoundly powerful.

Molly is a woman who has cultivated a presence in our neighborhood for the good of all. Loving people seems to come so naturally to her. I think we should all aspire to such greatness! I am constantly learning from her example. I learn so much from her whenever I am around her in the neighborhood. She is a beautiful cultivator of the communal imagination in our parish.

Macrina Wiederkkehr points out the importance of embracing the narrative of serving others when she says, "In this age when, unfortunately, many people appear to be caught in the limitations of individualism, how good to be reminded that we are called to serve others, not just ourselves."[7]

It may well be that individualism is limiting in ways that we have yet to discover. Individualism is a relational disability that scars our lives in subtle ways. When we take Christ's teachings seriously and become a servant to others, we open up a whole new way of imagining the body of Christ in everyday life together. We need others to help remind us that our imaginations are not captivated by the empire of North American culture, but that we are servants of others, that we possess a communal imagination for the place we inhabit together.

This is so crucial for our survival and sustainability. We need our lives to embody the communal imagination of becoming a servant to everyone we share life with. If we choose to ignore it, we will miss out on a meaningful life.

> When someone invites you to a wedding feast, do not take the place of honor, for a person more distinguished than you may have been invited. If so, the host who invited both of you will come and say to you, "Give this man your seat." Then, humiliated, you will have to take the least important place. But when you are invited, take the lowest place, so that when your host comes, he will say to you, "Friend, move up to a better place." Then you will be honored in the presence of all your fellow guests. For everyone who exalts himself will be humbled, and he who humbles himself will be exalted (Luke 14:8-11).

---

[7] Wiederkehr, *Seven Sacred Pauses*, 73.

Here is another example of Christ's teaching on humility and what becoming a servant to others means. He tells this parable to show us the importance of adopting a posture of humility in everyday life. If we assume we're worthy of sitting in the place of honor, we will be humiliated when told to get up and let someone who is genuinely worthy of that honor to sit there. Instead, if we choose for ourselves the least honorable seat, we might be invited to move to a better seat.

Christ wants us to choose the latter because it's what a truly humble person would do. If we were to take this teaching seriously, we would create in the parish an environment for all kinds of relational, collaborative revelations to occur among us. And the inner revolution that Dorothy Day spoke of earlier would constantly be shaping who we are becoming in our local context towards one another. Brian D. McLaren says, "Should we be surprised that Jesus said our role in this earth is not one of critics, cynics, escapists, controllers, or isolationists—but rather servants?"[8]

It is so easy to forget the more holistic identity of becoming great through becoming the servant of all. We are not called to be "critics." We are not called to be "cynics." We are not called to be "escapists." We are not called to be "controllers." We are not called to be "isolationists." What we are called to as the body of Christ together in everyday life is a communal imagination of relational humility and collaboration. And it is this that shapes us to become the servants of all in our local context. What a beautiful life this would be!

---

[8] McLaren, *More Ready than You Realize*, 148.

Part 5

The Abundance of Simplicity: Questioning Our Notions of Success

Chapter 12

Rethinking Consumerism: Confronting the Dominant Narrative of Upward Mobility

Reevaluating Ambition and Success: Recovering from Our Anxiousness

> People who want to get rich fall into temptation and a trap and into many foolish and harmful desires that plunge men into ruin and destruction. For the love of money is a root of all kinds of evil. Some people, eager for money, have wandered from the faith and pierced themselves with many griefs (1 Timothy 6: 9-10).

This Scripture ought to hit North Americans hard in the gut. Our whole way of life is founded on notions of ambition and success. The love of affluence and "greatness" through wealth has infiltrated our society to the point of insanity. We are on a trajectory of ruin and self-destruction. We are wandering from our faith and becoming a hyper-rootless people. We need to return to simplicity as a way of life. The gospel is rooted in the practice of simplicity in the place where we share life with others in. Simplicity is a part of the communal imagination. It subverts ambition and success. We act foolishly and we harm others when all we care about is ambition and success. Simplicity can save the body of Christ and help us to reconnect with one another and the place we inhabit together.

"If there is a religion that encompasses all the world," writes oblate Benedictine Kathleen Norris, "it is the pursuit of wealth."[1] The religion of the "pursuit of wealth" is destroying the body of Christ in North America and has left us blind to reality. This religion is all-consuming. It fosters master clichés and upholds the status quo. Many who are authentic about wanting to find what is real in life are becoming increasingly disillusioned with this kind of religion.

Our pursuit of ambition and success is defining the imagination of who we are becoming and it is leaving us pursuing our individualistic lifestyles disconnected from one another in everyday life. We end up not caring that much about neither place nor our relationships in the place that we live. Who has time for anyone else when we are chasing the pursuit of wealth?

What a lie we have believed! God weeps over North American culture with its lack of interest in simplicity, and striving instead for more wealth at the expense of others. Gus Gordon so eloquently says, "Money addiction goes way beyond the vital function it can perform and grows inside the personality like a cancer cell to such an extent all the faculties of the personality become devoted to its services. Bit by bit it corrupts every faculty we have. It twists our priorities and distorts our view of reality. In the end we forsake any authentic path to human fulfillment."[2]

We are so insecure that we cannot do without ambition and success. Our insecurities drown out the gospel. Our "money addiction" is murdering our imaginations like nothing we have ever seen before. This addiction is so powerful that we might think that this is the only path for us to follow.

---

[1] Norris, *Acadia and Me*, 128.

[2] Gordon, *Solitude and Compassion*, 152.

But the life of Christ in all its simplicity calls out to us and invites us to break free of this addiction. The simple life that he manifested will overrule the powerful religion of the pursuit of wealth. Christ is calling us to discern deeply our constant grasping for ambition and success. We need to look at how this is getting in the way of a simple life.

Our personalities are consumed mostly with dreams of ambition and success. We so easily become addicted to what money gives us: the power of autonomy, the ability to create our own lives apart from the community we live in. We want to escape our diversity and commonality and associate only with people who give us comfort and pleasure. This addiction to a religion of wealth will twist our priorities, confuse us as to what is real and what is illusion, and push us into abandoning any sense of authenticity.

Men especially are afraid of embracing simplicity. What else would they build their lives on if not ambition and success? They would have to find a new way to live their entire lives. And that's exactly what we need! We need to find and embody a new narrative and a new identity and stop playing games with fabricating our own false reality.

I am not saying that having money is completely bad. We all need a certain amount of money to live in this world. But what I am saying is that if our cravings for money possess us to the point of disregarding others and the place that we live, then, this is in no way the life Christ is calling us to. We need the freedom of simplicity that can give us back our time, our lives, our imaginations. The body of Christ is called to be functioning human beings with a communal imagination for simplicity in the place we inhabit together.

If the empire we live in can instill in us the status quo mindset of ambition and success, we will lose the revolutionary spirit of imagination. This is our culture's ultimate form of manipulation, and yet most of the time it has gone unnoticed. We become who the empire tells us to be. Where are the people who will not take this anymore and who will instead recreate their own lives through the Spirit of Christ?

Paulo Freire writes in his powerful book *The Pedagogy of the Oppressed*, "One of the methods of manipulation is to inoculate individuals with the bourgeois appetite for personal success."[3]

The pursuit of ambition and success always pulls us to somewhere we ought not to be. We live in a kind of disembodied state within our local context. We can never be truly present to others because we have our mind on getting somewhere else. We become totally utilitarian in the way we approach everyone and everything. We really don't care that much about our place. As long as things are going good, we really don't think of others that much. This is such an unhealthy way to live our lives. We need to find a better way. As long as we live in a paradigm of upward mobility, there will be very little hope for the body of Christ to share life together. The body of Christ will be fragmented because our eye is always on the next thing. Joan Chittister states,

> We run through the candy store of life always looking for the better job and the better pay and the better office. Nothing is ever good enough in the quest for success. Instead of settling down, we work constantly with one eye on the next office, the next opening, the next promotion. Instead of being who we are where we are, we are always on our way to somewhere else in this culture. So making friends with the neighbors is not a high priority. After all, we won't be here long.[4]

Our good friend Tom Sine of Mustard Seed Associates writes:, "Essentially the marketers of McWorld are seeking to convince adults everywhere on the planet to embrace a new definition of the good life as one of high status, high fashion and high living. We are invited to live into a story where we enjoy the luxurious lifestyles once reserved for the super-rich, whether we can afford it or not. And it is working."[5]

[3] Freire, *Pedagogy of the Oppressed*, 149.

[4] Chittister, *Wisdom Distilled from the Daily*, 91-92.

[5] Sine, *The New Conspirators*, 86-87.

The "new definition of the good life" that marketers spend millions of dollars on every year would have believe that ambition and success are virtues worth aspiring to. On the contrary, this pursuit of the "good life" is crippling our bodies and enslaving our imaginations. We lose our grip on simplicity as a hallmark of the body of Christ when we settle instead for a life of success.

"Success" is a strange term. These days it means single-mindedly pursuing a lifestyle where accruing material wealth matters more than generating social capital together. We become wrapped up with the need for more. As this "good life" is lived out, we become addicted to our wealth and create a religion around it. If we have any faith in God, we reduce God to what we want him to be, which usually amounts to a complete distortion of reality. Our imaginations also become distorted and we lose sight of one another in the process. This individualistic, consumeristic imagination and the communal imagination compete for our full attention, because they cannot coexist.

Our drive for ambition and success has made us a lonely and fragmented people. We have very little sense of togetherness anymore in our local context. "Moreover, the bonds that necessarily and beneficially connect us to each other, Norman Wirzba says, "have become weak and precarious, tenuous and provisional, because today's global marketplace requires people to be flexible, transient, rootless risk-takers who can seize whatever opportunity comes their way."[6]

The call of opportunity tends to push us away from one another in the parish. When we live more for personal economic gain rather than for relational connecting with one another in the place that we inhabit, we have lost our balance. We are going to have a hard fall if we do not change our ways. Our bonds are broken when we fail to nourish a discernment around simplicity. With our eyes fixed on new and better financial opportunities, we live into a transience that uproots us every couple of years. We never stay in a place long enough to develop

---

[6] Wirzba, *Living the Sabbath*, 65.

relationships of care. We never learn to see God through others because we are so quickly gone whenever something we perceive as better comes along. We need to really reflect on the effects of our ambition and success on those around us. Do we have the courage to replace it with a simplicity that draws us closer together as the body of Christ in the parish?

Ambition and success communicate that we do not need one another. We can make it on our own. We don't need to depend on anyone because we make our own things happen. This is an illusion. This kind of thinking and acting pulls us apart from one another in the parish. We begin to lose our souls

The body of Christ has been ripped apart by ambition and success. They are anything but countercultural. The communal imagination calls us out of this and into something more holistic. Bill McKibben writes in his book *Deep Economy*, "We don't need each other for anything anymore. If we have enough money, we're insulated from depending on those around us – which is at least as much a loss as a gain."[7] He goes on to say, "Our affluence isolates us ever more. We are not just individualists; we are hyper-individualists such as the world has never known."[8]

The worst kinds of injustices are done to others in the name of ambition and success. When we attach our imaginations and our identity to this way of being, we bring a lot of destruction down upon ourselves and others. "We really must understand," Quaker Richard J. Foster says, "that the lust for affluence in contemporary society is psychotic. It is psychotic because it has completely lost touch with reality."[9]

---

[7] McKibben, *Deep Economy*, 117.

[8] Ibid., 96.

[9] Foster, *Celebration of Discipline*, 80.

My friend Jay May is a good example of someone who has reevaluated ambition and success. He has stepped into an intentional simplicity in our neighborhood, freeing up his time to be more present and integrated in the community. Jay May used to be into a business where he made a lot of money. He had lots of nice things and found his identity in being successful. Most of his energy went into making money. He left it all behind when he was challenged with a new paradigm of being the body of Christ together with others in Downtown Tacoma. He heard the call and moved into a warehouse behind Tacoma Avenue where he worked on renovations with several friends. Together they created a shared living space where community initiatives could happen.

Jay May sold his car in order to walk more. He got a job as the director of the Farmer's Market in our neighborhood. Jay May became involved with the local politics of our Neighborhood Council. He also started a nonprofit organization called Local Life where he sells Christmas trees in the winter and holds neighborhood block parties in the summer.

Jay May focuses most of his energy now into building relationships in his local context. He loves to spend time with others and has profoundly simplified his life in order to do this. His example to all of us is amazing and I don't think he would ever go back to living an individualistic lifestyle of ambition and success. Jay May now loves being rooted in our neighborhood and partnering with his many friends there.

Considering the Abundance of Simplicity Over Consumerism: Re-orientating Our Entire Lives

Consumerism is a deadly poison that destroys simplicity among us. We become as addicted to it as a drug addict is addicted to heroine. We always want more and more. The cycle never ends and we are being pulled apart in the process to the point where there is very little togetherness anymore in everyday life. Consumerism plays on our very identity and imaginations. We have trouble seeing people as nothing more than mere objects to be manipulated and used for our own purposes. We stop caring when consumerism become our "drug of choice." Even our faith turns into a consumeristic product that we use for our own advantage when necessary. In such a mindset we lose all contact with reality, while continuing to believe that this is the "real world."

Simplicity is the practice that could help us free ourselves from all of this. There is a strength and wisdom in simplicity. God has given us simplicity as a guiding light in the darkness. Simplicity clarifies many things that are unknown to others. We are more open to the Spirit of Christ when simplicity is allowed to create life in us. Parker J. Palmer says:

> For many people, consumerism is the drug of choice for assuaging inner emptiness: we purchase goods and services not because we need them but because we think they will shore up our sense of identity and worth. The proof is close at hand in the ads that saturate our public and private lives, ads that rarely focus on the product's utility. Instead, they target the inner needs it allegedly fulfills, informed by market research on what consumers seek. 'Want to be youthful, beautiful, sophisticated, or powerful? Buy this!' Our addiction to consumption can run so deep that we keep buying these false promises for the life they give us, despite the fact that the temporary fix leaves us with emptier pocketbooks and still emptier hearts.[10]

What a mess our society has become. John McKnight and Peter Block say in their fascinating book *The Abundant Community*, "In our effort to find satisfaction through consumption, we are converted from citizen to consumer, and the implications of this are more profound than we realize."[11] When will we say that we will not play the game anymore? Our freedom would abound in a life of simplicity if we would take the risk.

---

[10] Palmer, *Healing the Heart of Democracy*, 63.

[11] McKnight and Block, *The Abundant Community*, 9.

We do not need to run the rat race and lose our life in the process. Christ has called us to be content in simplicity. Why don't we practice a theology of enough and give up on consumerism altogether? We would become more faithfully present in our locality if we just simply gave up consumerism to some extent. Consumerism is not open to a holistic spirituality in the parish. It wants nothing to do with it. Christopher L. Heuertz says in his book *Simple Spirituality*:

> In a culture saturated with overconsumption and gross materialism, it is hard not to believe this lie. The entire of humanity teaches us to live above our means, obtain things that we are unable to afford and living lifestyles that are not sustainable. So we spend more money to make ourselves feel better. Or we work harder and save more money so that our bank-account balances will provide us with a false sense of security. We make sure that our company provides us with the best retirement plan so that when we're old we can have 'enough' to be comfortable. We study to earn degrees, thinking they will define us and increase our marketable worth to the world. We try to keep up with the latest in fashion and entertainment so that we don't get "left behind." We move from one house to another, seeking out the bigger and better, all the while making sure that where we live is the "right" part of town or in the 'right' neighborhoods. We work hard to get ahead. The titles and positions are never enough, and so we sacrifice everything to move up the social or occupational ladder, desperately trying to "arrive." We give up who we truly are to try to become something we will never be. This becomes a habitual and destructive way of living. We're never free to celebrate what we have because we're always looking for what we can get and what we think we want or need.[12]

"I have come that they may have life, and have it to the full" (John 10:10). Christ offers us an abundant life in the fullness of simplicity. To have a full or abundant life does not mean consuming the narratives of the American dream. Instead, it means to be rich relationally in the place that we live. Christ desires for us a relational way of life that we his body facilitate by becoming his hands and feet to the world. This is

---

[12] Heuertz, *Simple Spirituality*, 57.

where the life of simplicity demonstrates its power. Simplicity brings us together in all kinds of ways. Without simplicity, we will not represent the body of Christ properly. Simplicity facilitates the creation of the communal imagination among us. We cannot afford to live addicted to consumerism any longer. Those days are over, and it is time for a new revolution of simplicity to begin within us in the parish.

The Holy Spirit is leading us into simplicity. The Spirit is bringing us together in relational ways as the body of Christ. Simplicity and the Spirit are collaborating to bring about relational revelations among us in everyday life together. What a beautiful thought!

The Holy Spirit is leading us to be citizens again, not consumers. Citizenship is about taking ownership of our lives together and not allowing the market forces to create our lives for us. We have gone through the twisted liturgies of consumption for so long that we have lost sight of one another in our lives. Simplicity is our only hope. Simplicity will stop the cycle of consumerism among us in the parish. It is important to practice simplicity for this very reason alone.

Consumerism is leading us down a path of seeing our faith as a commodity. It's what often defines our Christianity in North America: a bunch of abstract theological propositional statements disconnected from everyday life together. The body of Christ has become ineffectual and almost nonexistent in our local context because of our consumerism. The gospel doesn't even make sense to us anymore. No one can hear and understand the gospel when consumerism controls us. Vincent J. Miller says:

> Consumer culture forms people in consumerist habits of use and interpretation, which believers, in turn, bring to their religious beliefs and practice. Thus, while theology can offer daring and radical counternarratives by drawing on the rich wisdom of religious traditions, these responses are subject to the same fate as other cultural objects within consumer culture. For that reason, Christian counternarratives, metanarratives, or even master narratives are in danger of becoming ineffectual and, more than

that, of functioning as comforting delusions that are nothing more than a way for religious believers to convince themselves that, appearances notwithstanding, their religious faith is impervious to the erosions of commodification.[13]

I have always been drawn to simplicity. Having what I needed and not much more is how I have lived all of my life. I have never had large amounts of money. I have learned how to be content in every circumstance and to trust in God as the sustainer of my life. This has helped me to learn how to devote myself to my parish. In my local context, I have learned to live with what I need: the basic necessities of food, shelter, clothes and relational connection. My relationships are more important to me than my possessions, my economic status or anything else I may have.

Sometimes practicing simplicity is painful and there is a cost to it, but I am learning that even this plays a role in the shaping of our lives together. Our imaginations become freer. We have space to be faithfully present in our local context to love, listen, learn, and show empathy. I am learning that simplicity needs to be the priority in our lives if we are to be in genuine relationship with one another.

As I grew up, I really started to question life and how it works. I began to ask myself, "Why am I doing what I am doing?" I began to think about my motives and priorities. Questioning the pursuit of money and affluence was on my mind a lot. Thinking about how God fits into all of this was hard for me. Sometimes I remember feeling convicted over selfish acts that disregarded God and others. I began to ask, "Why aren't my motives in life and my priorities becoming more focused on others instead of myself?" I wondered what would happen if I embodied this more. I saw that the gospels had many stories and teachings on the importance of putting others first.

Reevaluating how I used my time became a common practice. Why was I watching so much TV? Why do I need so much stuff? Why am I so

---

13 Miller, *Consuming Religion*, 179.

obsessed with fashion and being cool? Why was everything so fast-paced? Why was I investing so much time in a social life with people who are like me and make me feel good? Why was I so into sports, movies and the internet? Why am I so focused on myself to the point of disregarding others? This didn't seem right to me, and so I started to center my life more on relational simplicity. I gave away things, changed priorities, and shifted focus. I became liberated from the imagination of the empire and started to move more toward the communal imagination.

When I first moved to Downtown Tacoma, I left my job as a teacher and took several jobs in the neighborhood where I made less money. This was a move that not many of my friends or family really understood. So I just did it without a lot of support from others. At first, I took a job as a dishwasher at a local restaurant. I also worked at a bar as a janitor and then as a parking lot attendant. All these jobs were within walking distance to where I was living the neighborhood. These jobs helped me to become more faithfully present and integrated in the parish. I developed lots of relationships when I really didn't know the neighborhood that well. This shaped me tremendously by helping me not to place such a high priority on the narratives of consumerism. Now I could focus on the relational context that I was in.

Simplicity is exemplified in the lives of the followers of Christ in the book of Acts. They lived to follow Christ. Christ himself chose a path of simplicity all his life. He taught that money and possessions were important tools to be used for the good of others.

The gospel can only be lived out in simplicity. Without simplicity it is too hard to live relationally with others in the parish. Our time and energy become consumed by the things we own. Relational revelations are stifled and ordinary miracles are smothered without some discernment around simplicity in our lives. Simplicity is essential to a life of faith together. In his book *The Freedom of Simplicity*, Richard J. Foster says, "The witness to simplicity is profoundly rooted in the biblical tradition, and most perfectly exemplified in the life of Jesus

Christ. In one form or another, all the devotional masters have stressed its essential nature. It is a natural and necessary outflow of the Good News of the Gospel having taken root in our lives."[14]

Is consumerism really "the real world'? Do we have to keep subjecting ourselves to this abusive system? Can there be an awakening to a different way of life together? Franciscan Richard Rohr observes, "If producing and consuming are the only games we play, they harden into our reality. Yes, it is a false reality, but it can grow more real to us as we grow older ... If we still believe that the system of producing and consuming is the real world, the only world, by the time we're fifty, there's almost no way out."[15]

I have always wondered why people usually mellow out into the status quo as they get older. I am coming to see that it is harder and harder to not get sucked into the temptation of affluence and consumerism. It is so common to believe the lie that we need to "grow up" and pursue "the responsible things" of adulthood, which usually means devoting most of our energy to an expensive mortgage and car payments along with many other pleasurable entertainments that we do not always need. When we have an overemphasis on such things, we lose touch with one another and the place that we live. Our lives become a manifestation of the individualistic status quo. Why do we need all this?

When we construct this "false reality" for ourselves, we are in the process of losing our souls to consumerism. And then this becomes the only reality we know with no chance for a communal imagination to develop among us. We can create our lives together into something more holistic as the body of Christ in the parish. We can give up the "religion of wealth" and become "atheists" of the dominant narrative of consumerism.

---

[14] Foster, *Freedom of Simplicity*, 4.

[15] Rohr, *Everything Belongs*, 63.

Rethinking Consumerism

John B. Hayes writes, "God desires to stretch before us a vision of living well—not simply living well off."[16] God wants us to live well together. We are to be more concerned with our relational connections than with our living well off in the hands of consumerism. God is wanting the communal imagination to flourish. Our love, grace, humility and simplicity need to work together as we seek to live well together over living well off individualistically.

We need to be free from the empire and the market which are not friendly toward anything that challenges the upward mobility of consumerism. Consumerism is the only way they can continue to exist as "the real world." God is dreaming about a new freedom that will leave us healed and whole. As Shane Claiborne and Chris Haw say, "God is in the work of liberating our imaginations from the clutches of the empire and market."[17]

---

[16] Hayes, *Sub-Merge*, 150.

[17] Claiborne and Haw, *Jesus for President*, 328.

Chapter 13

Redefining What Really Matters: The Integration of Everyday life

Slowing Down to Appreciate Life More: Opening Our Eyes to See

We live in such a fast-paced world that our lives cannot keep up. We have a hard time slowing down and creating new rhythms of a more peaceful way of life together. We take life and others for granted when we live at such high levels of speed. We cannot root ourselves in a place without first learning to slow down. We cannot be faithfully present to one another in our relationships without the simplicity of a slower pace that allows us to appreciate life more. Speed dominates our imaginations. It has crushed to pieces the communal imagination. We constantly disregard one another when we have no time just to be and reflect on what is going on within us.

Speed consumes every area of our lives. It damages us relationally in the parish. It makes us less than human. Speed can be addictive, just like consumerism. Rarely will we let go of our fast-paced life. But Christ is calling us to slow down and embrace one another more by adopting a lifestyle of simplicity that is subversive to speed. When will we see that our speed actually leads us nowhere fast? Christine Sine writes, "The quest for speed and efficiency dominates our modern lives, and everyone convinces us that this frenetic rhythm is the only one we can adopt—for every area of our lives."[1]

What is our speed accomplishing for us but more fragmentation and mental illness? It can never satisfy our feelings of emptiness. It keeps us from looking deep within ourselves. We fear emptiness and pain, so we live at a faster and faster pace in a desperate bid to avoid facing ourselves and others in the parish. Speed has us moving around so fast that no one will ever get to know us very well. Speed is about protecting our security and defending our preferred lifestyle. We disregard everyone else and become apathetic about anything of value in life when the pace of life is all that matters. Speed and individualism go hand in hand, making life together nonexistent. Speed is co-opting our imaginations

I think of my friend Ben, who's learned to slow down so he can appreciate life more. Ben loves to take trips out into nature and just soak in the connectedness of everything around him. It is calming for him to observe the mountains, oceans, waves, wind, and sand. It helps him rediscover a sense of perspective. In the process, he is growing and constantly changing, as his times of solitude make him more aware of his need for an authentic spirituality. Ben has come to a deep sense of gratitude and a love of life as it is.

Ben practices meditation a lot to help him deal with the speed of life. This is not just something Ben does in the morning for a set period of time. It is a way of life that cannot be separated from his relationships in community. Ben has a longing that his meditation practice will affect everything he does in life. Meditation invites reflection and listening within. It cultivates in Ben love, compassion, hope, and awareness of the world around him.

Ben also loves to run and hike. Running is a very meditative act for Ben. It takes him to the present moment where his mind is open and

---

[1] Sine, *Sacred Rhythms*, 29.

he is aware of his body. He becomes deeply conscious of movement in and around him, his heart rate and his breathing. When Ben goes hiking, he loses all sense of time. The calendar and his schedule become irrelevant to him. He likes to get out into a part of nature where he can feel the wind on his face and be mindful of his feet on the ground. As a hiker, Ben is becoming mindful of the sacredness of the earth.

"How hard it is for the rich to enter the kingdom of God! Indeed, it is easier for a camel to go through the eye of a needle than for a rich man to enter the kingdom of God" (Luke 18:24-25). Our speed has everything to do with a desire for wealth, status, and the American dream. When we live at high levels of speed, we are being driven more by self-centered personal material gain than by any desire for the collective good of others in our neighborhood. In this Scripture, Christ is teaching us that those addicted to wealth and speed have a hard time understanding the kingdom of God. They have a hard time seeing anything authentic, because they don't have the right posture to listen and understand. They are out of control. This is a major crisis within the body of Christ in the twenty-first century.

Our spirits are not healthy when speed dominates all of life. "There is a connection between our speed and the health of our spirits,"[2] Leighton Ford says in his book *The Attentive Life*. Our spirits were never meant to live this way. Speed makes us dizzy, but we keep going anyway. This fast-paced life is making us sick and dysfunctional.

Our speed is ruining the body of Christ in the parish. The pursuit of the religion of wealth with ambition, success and consumerism as the guiding lights, is pulling us in all directions.

Our salvation has something to say about our speed. Can salvation and speed co-exist? Mark Scrandrette notes, "Our pace of life affects our capacity to appreciate the goodness of God. We may simply be too busy or distracted to notice and receive the bounty that surrounds us. The

---

[2] Ford, *The Attentive Life*, 105.

demands of a hurried life and the dominance of technology cloud our awareness. Slowing down and learning to pay attention to the moment may be a path to affirming God's essential goodness."[3]

God is so good to us in everyday life, but many times we cannot see it because we are blinded by speed and our mobility. Speed does not allow for any faithful presence to one another in the parish. It is only when we slow down to appreciate life more that we can begin to rediscover God's essential goodness through one another. The place we inhabit becomes the medium of God's goodness to us in all kinds of ways. We begin to find relational revelations in the most unexpected places. Slowing down and paying attention to the moments we spend with others may be the most revolutionary thing we could possibly do.

Speed is the modern invention of life that imprisons our imaginations and steals our lives. It is a key component of the same empire that promotes consumerism, ambition, and success. Speed promotes colonialism within the body of Christ. But when we slow down and listen, our simplicity subverts colonialism. We can learn to listen well enough to be shaped within instead of always trying to change others. We can learn to become more peaceful as we build trust with others. Richard Mahler states, "When we move slower, we see what otherwise passes by in a blur. When we really listen, we hear what arises within."[4]

Our lives are so fast-paced that we have lost sight of our salvation. We have reduced it to a bunch a propositional statements or theological ideas that are disconnected from place and living well together in everyday life. Ian Adams, director of Stillpoint, a project seeking to nurture spiritual practice says, "Contemporary life, for most of us, is lived at a fast pace. And Christianity has not always offered its best learning and practice to those of us in thrall to speed."[5] Christianity and speed cannot co-exist. If we are committed to speed we will soon

---

[3] Scandrette, *Soul Graffiti*, 93.

[4] Mahler, *Stillness*, 81.

[5] Adams, *Cave Refectory Road*, 41.

become invisible to one another in the parish. Our relationships cannot survive our speed. Carl Honore in his book *In Praise of Slowness* says:

> The problem is that our love of speed, our obsession with doing more and more in less and less time, has gone too far; it has turned into an addiction, a kind of idolatry. Even when speed starts to backfire, we invoke the go-faster gospel ... And yet some things cannot, should not, be sped up. They take time; they need slowness. When you accelerate things that should not be accelerated, when you forget how to slow down, there is a price to pay.[6]

Idolizing what Honore calls the "go-faster gospel" has its consequences. It makes us extremely disconnected from one another. It will not allow us to become rooted in a place. This needs to change if the body of Christ is ever to become relevant once more in the parish. We need the freedom of simplicity to slow us down and give us back our sanity.

"What good is it for a man to gain the whole world, yet forfeit his soul? Or what can a man give in exchange for his soul?" (Mark 8:36-37). We are losing our souls to speed. Our speed is our slavery. But Christ has come to set the captives free. Christ wants to give us the freedom to inhabit a place without speed. He wants us to have a lasting connection with one another. "We do not want to disappear. If we slow down," Wayne Muller states, "we might be pulled by some gravity to the bottom of our feelings, we might drown in all we have lost. So we keep moving, never finding refuge, never touching the tenderness that propel us into a life of speedy avoidance."[7]

We have no trouble avoiding and escaping anything we do not want to face in everyday life. It seems we have mastered this technique quite well. It is even accepted as perfectly normal within Christianity these days. But the truth is we are terrified to slow down because if we did, all the clichés we hold onto so tightly in the name of Christianity might be

---

[6] Honore, *In Praise of Slowness*, 4-5.

[7] Muller, *Sabbath*, 53.

shown for what they are: a prefabricated answer that keeps us safe from taking any responsibility in life.

When I first started to risk slowing down my life, it was hard. But now after many years of practicing simplicity I find it has brought me peace. It is so nice not to have the pressure of speed to push me around. I can reject the "go-faster gospel" and I can trust that my relationships are much more important than a life of speed, ambition, wealth, and achievement. If people call me "irresponsible" because I have opted out of a speed-driven life, that is okay. I am learning to be rooted in my neighborhood and becoming content with practicing simplicity.

My identity is wrapped up in learning to have the time to appreciate life more through taking walks in my neighborhood. Walking down the streets of Downtown Tacoma and running into friends wherever I go is something I love to experience. I come alive on these kinds of spontaneous connections. Being able to slow down to read, reflect, and write at a local coffee shop is so valuable to me. I enjoy having the time to spend with others at dinners and lunches. I always connect well with others in these environments because I have learned to be faithfully present. Going running in my neighborhood while listening to music that helps me to think about life relaxes me. To be outside and feel the sun on my face and watch the birds perching on a ledge or flying away into the sky is a beautiful feeling. I love having the freedom to appreciate others and greet them as we pass by through the course of a day.

We can never be faithfully present right where we are when we're addicted to speed. We move at such a fast pace through life that we cannot experience anything wonderful anymore. Barbara Brown Taylor writes, "Most of us move so quickly that our surroundings become no more than the blurred scenery we fly past on our way to somewhere else."[8] We need to stop doing damage to others and slow down in order to be present to one another again. God is found in slowing down

---

[8] Taylor, *An Altar in the World*, 24.

through a way of life that advocates simplicity, proximity, locality, and relational connection to one another.

Finding Value in What Matters: Having the Courage to Discover Ourselves

It takes courage to simplify our lives. It takes courage to search for and enter into a lifelong process of discovery about what really matters in everyday life. This process of discovery is relational. It is embodied in the place that we live. Without simplicity, we will not be able to connect very well either to God or to one another. Richard J. Foster notes, "As we strive for simplicity we take energy away from the direction the world is heading and refocus it on a new, life-giving vision for living together. Simplicity engenders new values which bring about new decisions which brings about a new society."[9]

What will people think if we live a life of simplicity? We might stand out too much and become something other than the status quo. But it is worth the risk. When we embrace simplicity, it will shape us in ways we cannot understand. Simplicity redefines everyday life and all our relationships. It helps us to become integrated into the communal imagination. Thomas Merton writes, "Without courage we can never attain to true simplicity."[10]

Our place and our everyday relationships in that place are what really matter in life. This is so integral to our spirituality. Without a theology of place, we cannot live into the courage of simplicity and embrace a holistic counterculture. Simplicity is not necessarily an act of ethics or morality, but rather an act of courage. Courage is everything to our spirituality. It takes courage to be in relationship with others. It takes courage to forsake the status quo and be creative with our everyday lives. It takes courage to see life through the eyes of beauty and simplicity. It takes courage to become rooted in a place. When we

---

[9] Foster, *Freedom of Simplicity*, 201.

[10] Merton, *Thoughts in Solitude*, 34.

intentionally practice simplicity, we draw energy away from the individualistic, consumeristic thrust of society and create a new synergy. Simplicity empowers us to imagine a life that is not bound to the North American status quo lifestyle. "To this end I labor, struggling with all his energy, which so powerfully works in me" (Colossians 1:29). This energy of simplicity is about finding value in what truly matters so that society can still remain beautiful. What hope is there for society if there is no return to simplicity? What hope is there for us without beauty in the world? What hope is there if everyday life should lose all its value? Simplicity could save our civilization. Maybe we could be the ones who preserve some value and beauty in life.

"Finally, brothers, whatever is true, whatever is noble, whatever is right, whatever is pure, whatever is lovely, whatever is admirable—if anything is excellent or praiseworthy—think about such things" (Philippians 4:8). There is no way we can think about such things unless we practice simplicity, because without it, we will never be attentive to everyday life. Only in simplicity are we able to discern what is noble, right, pure, lovely, admirable and excellent in others. Only in simplicity can we once more begin to see our place as beautiful and sacred and God's gift to us. Only in simplicity do we stop taking others for granted. Mark Scandrette, who has lived in the Mission District of San Francisco for over a decade, says, "The quest for simplicity and contentment, rather than being legislated by rules, can be guided by a question: "How can I manage my life to be the most free to hear the voice of love?" You will find the best rhythm of simplicity through careful experimentation."[11]

What this "careful experimentation" looks like will depend on your particular context. Maybe it looks like renting a home instead of taking out a mortgage to buy one. Maybe it looks like buying a cheaper home so you don't have to work fifty or sixty hours a week to pay for a bigger one. Maybe it has to do with trading in your car for a cheaper one. Maybe it has to do with getting rid of your car altogether and working at a job in the neighborhood instead of commuting to a job outside the

---

[11] Scandrette, *Soul Graffiti*, 215.

neighborhood. Maybe it has to do with taking a pay cut in order to work at a job that you enjoy more. Maybe it has to do with walking or biking more in the neighborhood. Maybe it has to do with getting rid of your entertainment devices so you can spend more time with people. Maybe it has to do with simplifying your wardrobe. Maybe it has to do with abstaining from certain social events or monitoring what you eat and drink. Maybe it has to do with buying less stuff. Maybe it has to do with practicing media fasts.

There are countless examples that could be cited. Probably no two people will make exactly the same decisions. The important thing is that we have the courage to enter into a process of discovering how to embody simplicity so we can again listen to our lives and connect with others. This will constantly evolve as we go through different stages of life. God will always reveal what steps we need to take to simplify our lives.

> The ground of a certain rich man produced a good crop. He thought to himself, "What shall I do? I have no place to store my crops."
>
> Then he said, "This is what I'll do. I will tear down my barns and build bigger ones, and there I will store my grain and my goods." And I'll say to myself, "You have plenty of good things laid up for many years. Take life easy; eat, drink and be merry."
>
> But God said to him, "You fool! This very night your life will be demanded from you. Then who will get what you have prepared for yourself?"
>
> This is how it will be with anyone who stores up things for himself but is not rich toward God (Luke 12:16-21).

Our practice of simplicity will cause us to be rich relationally towards our neighbors in the parish. We must not store up things for ourselves at the expense of connecting with others. Christ says to forsake simplicity is foolishness. Word Made Flesh co-director Christopher L. Heuertz writes: "Simplicity is best understood in evaluating how we hold things."[12] Do we hold things with open or closed hands? Do we use the things that we own to benefit ourselves or to bless others? Do we embrace simplicity in our relationships or do we push it away? Is a discernment surrounding simplicity a part of our spirituality? We cannot live into the communal imagination without simplicity.

My friend Liz has been exploring simplicity for quite some time now, and this has led her to greater authenticity. When she was younger, she was quiet and submissive. But now that has all changed, since she moved into our neighborhood. With a lot of encouragement from her husband Paul, Liz now desires that all woman be empowered to discover themselves and the courage to be who they are. She believes that this is absolutely crucial for everyday life with others. Liz is not content with being quiet and submissive anymore. She wants to be her authentic self. She feels we find ourselves when we pay close attention to the voices of others in the community.

Liz has had to constantly ask herself, "What do I want out of life?" She used to want the typical American dream of a house with a white picket fence, but now she feels that our homes need to be used to connect with others in the community. Liz desires that we share what we own for the sake of being together in the parish. She wants to spend more time with people in the neighborhood. For Liz, life is less about owning things for her own wellbeing and more about relationships and restoration. It is about having less and treating the things she does have with care, including her household possessions such as a couch or a dining room table. According to Liz, we are all called to be good stewards of what God has given us for the benefit of others. This is a radical transformation from what Liz used to value in our North American culture.

Every one of us is called to be discerning about what simplicity looks like in their own lives. It will look different for each one of us, but regardless we all must live in simplicity if we are to be the body of

---

[12] Heuertz, *Simple Spirituality*, 90.

Christ in the parish. There is no way around this. So much of what Christ teaches will be impossible to follow if we do not embody simplicity in our everyday lives together. Without simplicity, we cannot find value in what matters in life. Nor will we discover the true value of relationships. Without simplicity, we will become so busy doing our own thing that all the meaningful things in life become secondary. When we seek simplicity is when we begin to seek God in holistic ways.

Simplicity gives us the capacity to find room in our lives for what will bring strength and stability to the parish. Simplicity could become our greatest source of freedom as we share life together. We are all called to simplicity no matter who we are. Simplicity brings a broader perspective to social justice issues in the place that we live. It teaches us to handle our relationships more justly and to treat others with equality. Through simplicity no one is better than anyone else and our economic status is shown for the false narrative that it is.

We have allowed our consumerism to blind our imaginations to place. We run around with our money and things in hopes of escaping a shared life with others with whom we ought to be in solidarity. Our all-consuming wealth has left us lonely and isolated. We have settled for something less. When there is no holistic counterculture rooted in community, this is all we have. Joan Chittister writes, "We accumulate all our lives and carry the things around with us until we have spent more time and money on things than we have on living."[13]

We prefer to focus on all the things that promote financial wealth, affluence, and power, while focusing much less on what promotes true life together. "Living together" has been reduced in meaning to refer to just two or more people living under the same roof. We need to more broadly imagine what living together in the parish in simplicity might look like. We need to value what matters in everyday life.

---

[13] Chittister, *Wisdom Distilled from the Daily*, 74.

We have pursued and used our time and money solely for our own ends to the point that we no longer have any connection to what is real. We have objectified almost everything and our spirituality is mostly just empty words which have very little to do with sharing everyday life together in a particular place. That is a sad substitute for living life together in the parish.

Bibliography

Adams, Ian. *Cave Refectory Road: Monastic Rhythms for Contemporary Living*. London: Canterbury Press Norwich, 2010.

Barry, William A. *Letting God Come Close: An Approach to the Ignatian Spiritual Exercises*. Chicago: Loyola Press, 2001.

Barton, Ruth Haley. *Sacred Rhythms: Arranging Our Lives for Spiritual Transformation*. Downers Grove: InterVarsity, 2006.

Benner, David G. *Sacred Companions: The Gift of Spiritual Friendship and Direction*. Downers Grove: InterVarsity, 2002.

Berry, Wendell. *Sex, Economy, Freedom and Community*. New York: Pantheon, 1993.

Bonhoeffer, Dietrich. *Life Together*. New York: HarperSanFrancisco, 1954.

_____. *The Cost of Discipleship*. New York: Touchstone, 1995.

Brewin, Kester. *Signs of Emergence: A Vision for Church that is Organic/ Networked/Decentralized/ Bottom-Up/ Communal/ Flexible {Always Evolving}*. Grand Rapids: Baker, 2007.

Carretto, Carlo. *Letters from The Desert*. Maryknoll: Orbis, 1972.

Casey, Michael. *Toward God: The Ancient Wisdom of Western Prayer*. Liguori: Liguori/Triumph, 1996.

Cavey, Bruxy. *The End of Religion: Encountering the Subversive Spirituality of Jesus*. Colorado Springs: NavPress, 2007.

Chittister, Joan. *Wisdom Distilled from the Daily: Living the Rule of St. Benedict Today.* New York: HarperOne, 1991.

Christensen, Michael J. and Rebecca J. Laird. *Henri Nouwen: Spiritual Direction: Wisdom for the Walk of Faith.* New York: HarperSanFrancisco, 2006.

————. *Henri Nouwen: Spiritual Formation: Following the Movements of the Spirit* New York: HarperOne, 2010.

Claiborne, Shane. *The Irresistible Revolution: Living as an Ordinary Radical.* Grand Rapids: Zondervan, 2006.

———— and Chris Haw, *Jesus for President: Politics for Ordinary Radicals.* Grand Rapids: Zondervan, 2008.

———— and John M. Perkins. *Follow Me to Freedom: Leading and Following as an Ordinary Radical.* Ventura: Regal, 2009.

———— and Jonathan Wilson-Hartgrove. *Becoming the Answer to Our Prayers: Prayer for Ordinary Radicals.* Downers Grove: InterVarsity, 2008.

Day, Dorothy. *Loaves and Fishes: The Inspiring Story of the Catholic Worker Movement.* Maryknoll: Orbis, 1997.

————. *On Pilgrimage.* Grand Rapids: Eerdmans, 1999.

————. *The Long Loneliness: The Autobiography of the Legendary Catholic Social Activist.* New York: HarperCollins, 1997.

Dekar, Paul R. *Community of the Transfiguration: The Journey of a New Monastic Community.* Eugene: Cascade, 2008.

Delio, Ilia. *Franciscan Prayer.* Cincinnati: St. Anthony Messenger, 2004.

De Waal, Esther. *Lost in Wonder: Rediscovering the Spiritual Art of Attentiveness.* Collegeville: Liturgical, 2003.

Dickau, Tim. *Plunging into the Kingdom Way: Practicing the Shared Strokes of Community, Hospitality, Justice, and Confession.* Eugene: Cascade, 2011.

Doherty, Catherine. *Poustinia: Encountering God in Silence, Solitude and Prayer.* Combermere: Madonna House, 2000.

Ellis, June, "Growing Together in Community." In *Plain Living: A Quaker Path to Simplicity*, edited by Catherine Whitmire et al., 145. Notre Dame: Sorin, 2001.

Ellul, Jacques. *The Subversion of Christianity.* Grand Rapids: Eerdmans, 1986.

Farrington, Debra K. *Living Faith Day By Day: How the Sacred Rules of Monastic Traditions Can Help You Live Spiritually in the Modern World.* New York: Perigee, 2000.

Feiss, Hugh. *Essential Monastic Wisdom: Writings on the Contemplative Life.* New York: HarperSanFrancisco, 1999.

Finely, James. *Christian Meditation: Experiencing the Presence of God.* New York: HarperSanFrancisco, 2004.

Ford, Leighton. *The Attentive Life: Discerning the Presence Of God in All Things.* Downers Grove: InterVarsity, 2008.

Foster, Richard J. *Celebration of Discipline: The Path to Spiritual Growth.* New York: HarperSanFrancisco, 1998.

_____. *Freedom of Simplicity: Finding Harmony in a Complex World.* New York: HarperSanFrancisco, 2005.

Freire, Paulo. *Pedagogy of the Oppressed.* New York: The Continuum International, 2009.

Friesen, Dwight J. *Thy Kingdom Connected: What the Church Can Learn from Facebook, the Internet, and Other Networks.* Grand Rapids: Baker, 2009.

_____. "Formation in the Post-Christendom Era." In *The Gospel After Christendom: New Voices, New Cultures, New Expressions,* edited by Ryan K. Bolger et al., 203. Grand Rapids: Baker Academic, 2012.

Frost, Michael. *Jesus the Fool: The Mission of the Unconventional Christ.* Peabody: Hendrickson, 2010.

_____. *Seeing God in the Ordinary: A Theology of the Everyday.* Peabody: Hendrickson, 2000.

_____ and Alan Hirsch. *ReJesus: A Wild Messiah for a Missional Church.* Peabody: Hendrickson, 2009.

_____ and Alan Hirsch. *The Faith of Leap: Embracing a Theology of Risk, Adventure and Courage.* Grand Rapids: Baker, 2011.

_____ and Alan Hirsch. *The Shaping of Things to Come: Innovation and Mission for the 21st Century Church.* Peabody: Hendrickson, 2003.

Fryling, Alice. *Seeking God Together: An Introduction to Group Spiritual Direction.* Downers Grove: InterVaristy, 2009.

Gibbs, Eddie. *Leadership Next: Changing Leaders in a Changing Culture.* Downers Grove: InterVarsity, 2005.

Bibliography

Gordon, Gus. *Solitude and Compassion: The Path to the Heart of the Gospel.* Maryknoll: Orbis, 2009.

Grout, Marius. "Growing Together in Reconciliation and Forgiveness." In *Plain Living: A Quaker Path to Simplicity*, edited by Catherine Whitmire et al., 159. Notre Dame: Sorin, 2001.

Hayes, John B. *Sub-Merge: Living Deep in a Shallow World: Service, Justice and Contemplation Among The World's Poor.* Ventura: Regal, 2006.

Heath, Elaine A., and Scott T. Kisker. *Longing for Spring: A New Vision for Wesleyan Community.* Eugene: Cascade, 2010.

Heuertz, Christopher L. *Simple Spirituality: Learning to See God in a Broken World.* Downers Grove: InterVarsity, 2008.

_____ and Christine D. Pohl. *Friendship at the Margins: Discovering Mutuality in Service and Mission.* Downers Grove: InterVarsity, 2010.

Honore, Carl. *In Praise of Slowness: Challenging the Cult of Speed.* New York: HarperSanFrancisco, 2004.

Houston, James M. *The Prayer: Deepening Your Friendship with God.* Colorado Springs: Victor, 2007.

Huston, Paula. *The Holy Way: Practices for a Simple Life.* Chicago: Loyola Press, 2003.

Imbach, Jeff. *The River Within: Loving God, Living Passionately.* Colorado Springs: NavPress, 1998.

Johnson, Jan. *Invitation to the Jesus Life: Experiments in Christlikeness.* Colorado Springs: NavPress, 2008.

Keating, Thomas. *Invitation to Love: The Way of Christian Contemplation.* New York: The Continuum International, 2004.

Keel, Tim. *Intuitive Leadership: Embracing a Paradigm of Narrative, Metaphor and Chaos.* Grand Rapids: Baker, 2007.

Kempis, Thomas a. *The Imitation of Christ.* New York: Vintage, 1998.

Kent, Keri Wyatt. *Listen: Finding God in the Story of Your Life.* San Francisco: Jossey-Bass, 2006.

Kidder, Annemarie S. *The Power of Solitude: Discovering Your True Self in a World of Nonsense and Noise.* New York: The Crossroad, 2007.

King Jr., Martin Luther. *Strength to Love.* Philadelphia: Fortress, 1983.

Laird, Martin. *Into the Silent Land: A Guide to the Christian Practice of Contemplation.* New York: Oxford University Press, 2006.

Mahler, Richard. *Stillness: Daily Gifts of Solitude.* Boston: Red Wheel, 2003.

McKibben, Bill. *Deep Economy: The Wealth of Communities and the Durable Future.* New York: Times, 2007.

McKnight, John and Peter Block. *The Abundant Community: Awakening the Power of Families and Neighborhoods.* San Francisco: Berrett-Koehler, 2010.

McLaren, Brian. *Finding Our Way Again: The Return of the Ancient Practices.* Nashville: Thomas Nelson, 2008.

_____. *More Ready than You Realize: The Power of Everyday Conversations.* Grand Rapids: Zondervan, 2006.

Meek, Esther Lightcap. *Loving to Know: Covenant Epistemology.* Eugene: Cascade, 2011.

Meninger, William A. *The Loving Search for God: Contemplative Prayer and the Cloud of Unknowing.* New York: The Continuum International, 1994.

Merton, Thomas. *Life and Holiness.* Garden City: Image, 1964.

_____. *New Seeds of Contemplation.* New York: New Direction, 1961.

_____. *No Man is an Island.* Orlando: Harcourt Brace & Company, 1983.

_____. *Thoughts in Solitude.* New York: Farrar, Straus & Giroux, 1986.

Miller, Vincent J. *Consuming Religion: Christian Faith and Practice in a Consumer Culture.* New York: The Continuum International, 2003.

Mulholland Jr., M. Robert. *Invitation to a Journey: A Road Map for Spiritual Formation.* Downers Grove: InterVarsity, 1993

_____. *The Deeper Journey: The Spirituality of Discovering Your True Self.* Downers Grove: InterVarsity, 2006.

Muller, Wayne. *Sabbath: Finding Rest, Renewal, and Delight in Our Busy Lives.* New York: Bantom, 1999.

Nelson, Alan E. *Embracing Brokenness: How God Refines Us Through Life's Disappointments.* Colorado Springs: NavPress, 2002.

Nhat Hanh, Thich. *Touching Peace: Practicing the Art of Mindfulness.* Berkley: Parallax, 1992.

Norris, Gunilla. *Inviting Silence: Universal Principles of Meditation.* New York: BlueBridge, 2004.

Norris, Kathleen. *Acadia and Me: A Marriage, Monks, and a Writer's Life.* New York: Riverhead, 2008.

Nouwen, Henri. *Reaching Out: The Three Movements of the Spiritual Life.* New York: Image, 1975.

O' Keefe, John. *BoneYARD: Creatives Will Change the Way We Lead in the Church.* Sacramento: DeadFish, 2010.

Okoro, Enuma. *Reluctant Pilgrim: A Moody, Somewhat Self-Indulgent Introvert's Search for Spiritual Community.* Nashville: Fresh Air, 2010.

Palmer, Parker J. *A Hidden Wholeness: The Journey Toward an Undivided Life.* San Francisco: Jossey-Bass, 2004.

————. *Healing the Heart of Democracy: The Courage to Create a Politics Worthy of the Human Spirit.* San Francisco: Jossey-Bass, 2011.

————. *The Courage to Teach: Exploring the Inner Landscape of a Teacher's Life.* San Francisco: Jossey-Bass, 1998.

Percy, Walker. *Signposts in a Strange Land.* New York: Picador, 1991.

Rohr, Richard. *Everything Belongs: The Gift of Contemplative Prayer.* New York: The Crossroad, 2003.

————. *Simplicity: The Freedom of Letting Go.* New York: The Crossroad, 2003.

————. *The Naked Now: Learning to See as the Mystics See.* New York: The Crossroad, 2009.

————. *Things Hidden: Scripture as Spirituality.* Cincinnati: St. Anthony Messenger, 2008.

Rolheiser, Ronald. *The Holy Longing: The Search for a Christian Spirituality.* New York: Doubleday, 1999.

Roxburgh, Alan J. *Missional: Joining God in the Neighborhood.* Grand Rapids: Baker, 2011.

Scandrettte, Mark. *Practicing the Way of Jesus: Life Together in the Kingdom of Love.* Downers Grove: InterVarsity, 2011.

————. *Soul Graffiti: Making a Life in the Way of Jesus.* San Francisco: Jossey- Bass, 2007.

Schlabach, Gerald W. *Unlearning Protestantism: Sustaining Christian Community in an Unstable Age.* Grand Rapids: Brazos, 2010.

Shannon, William. *Silence on Fire: Prayer of Awareness*. New York: The Crossroad, 2000.

Shaw, Luci. *Breath for the Bones: Art, Imagination, and Spirit: Reflections on Creativity and Faith*. Nashville: Thomas Nelson, 2007.

Simsic, Wayne. *Thomas Merton: An Invitation to the Contemplative Life*. Ijamsville: The Word Among Us, 2006.

Sine, Christine. *Sacred Rhythms: Finding a Peaceful Pace in a Hectic World*. Grand Rapids: Baker, 2003.

Sine, Tom. *The New Conspirators: Creating the Future One Mustard Seed at a Time*. Downers Grove: InterVarsity, 2008.

Steindl-Rast, David. *Gratefulness, The Heart of Prayer: An Approch to Life in Fullness*. Mahwah: Paulist, 1984.

Stern, Anthony. *Everything Starts from Prayer: Mother Teresa's Meditations on Spiritual Life for People of All Faiths*. New Delhi: Full Circle, 2007.

Taylor, Barbara Brown. *An Altar in the World: A Geography of Faith*. New York: HarperOne, 2009.

Thibodeaux, Mark E. *Armchair Mystic: Easing into Contemplative Prayer*. Cincinnati: St. Anthony Messenger, 2001.

Walsch, Brian J. and Sylvia C. Keesmaat. *Colossians Remixed: Subverting the Empire*. Downers Grove: InterVarsity, 2004.

Weil, Simone. *Waiting For God*. New York: HarperCollins, 2001.

Wiederkehr, Macrina. *A Tree Full of Angels: Seeing the Holy in the Ordinary*. New York: HarperSanFrancisco, 1990.

_____. *Seven Sacred Pauses: Living Mindfully Through the Hours of the Day*. Notre Dame: Sorin, 2008.

Willard, Dallas. *Renovation of the Heart: Putting on the Character of Christ*. Colorado Springs: NavPress, 2002.

Wilson-Hartgrove, Jonathan. *God's Economy: Redefining the Health and Wealth Gospel*. Grand Rapids: Zondervan 2009.

Wirzba, Norman. *Living the Sabbath: Discovering the Rhythms of Rest and Delight*. Grand Rapids: Brazos, 2006.

Bibliography

About the Author

Mark Votava lives in the Pacific Northwest in Tacoma, Washington where he has rooted himself in the neighborhood of Downtown Tacoma having become a local practitioner of faithful presence since 2004. He has been a part of the Downtown Neighborhood Fellowship for over a decade and has been a core member of the Tacoma Catholic Worker since 2010 where he shares life with the poor, marginalized and oppressed. He has dedicated his life to exploring and practicing a more subversive, creative, innovative way of life in the twenty-first century that is engaged relationally in the place he lives. Striving to help others create a new paradigm of ecclesiology through the embodiment of parish, Mark collaborates with the Parish Collective Leaders Fellowship and has graduated from the Leadership in the New Parish course at the Seattle School of Theology and Psychology.

Website // markvotava.com
Twitter // @MarkVotava

About Urban Loft Publishers

Urban Loft Publishers focuses on ideas, topics, themes, and conversations about all things urban. Renewing the city is the central theme and focus of what we publish. It is our intention to blend urban ministry, theology, urban planning, architecture, urbanism, stories, and the social sciences, as ways to drive the conversation. We publish a wide variety of urban perspectives, from books by the experts about the city to personal stories and personal accounts of urbanites who live in the city.

Other Books by ULP

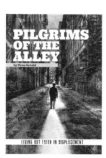

Pilgrims of the Alley
Living Out Faith in Displacement
Dave Arnold

Sometimes people wonder why they feel stuck in life, as if they are living out their days in an unnatural and often hostile environment. The truth is, this is a reality for people attempting to follow Jesus in our world. We are displaced persons. To be displaced means to be away from or out of one's natural environment. And I believe it's in this environment our faith grows the most. Why? Because God is at work in displacement, and it's in this environment—in the alleys of life—where extraordinary growth takes place and our faith grows the most. This book is about a journey of understanding how we are to navigate a life of faith amid a world of such uncertainty, of darkness, and oftentimes, of great despair.

"Dave aptly slips on the shoes of the pilgrim and walks their journey through displacement. *Pilgrims of the Alley* will surprise, console, and encourage those already on the journey, and also those who choose to slip on pilgrim shoes to strengthen their own faith. It's personal, biblically-anchored, and absolutely inspirational. I highly recommend it."

Stephan J. Bauman
President & CEO, World Relief

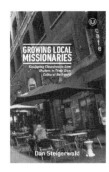

Growing Local Missionaries
Equipping Churches to Sow Shalom in Their Own Cultural Backyard
Dan Steigerwald

Growing Local Missionaries is about real action for the good of the world—equipping people to move in their neighborhoods and cities with confidence in both their God-given identity and their capacity to pass on practical missionary skills.

"Wow! This little book is jam-packed full of practical wisdom. Dan helps us engage our world as agents of shalom, providing achievable steps to make a real difference in our cities and neighborhoods. I loved it!"

Deb Hirsch
Conference speaker for Forge (www.forgeamerica.com); church leader in Tribe of LA; co-author, *Untamed: Reactivating a Missional Form of Discipleship.*

"In the midst of the church's confusion and discouragement today, this book offers a lifeline of hope and praxis that actually works. Armed with a set of well-worn practices and a strong biblical framing, Dan helps the reader expand their horizons of imagination and engagement within their own community. This is a gem!"

Deborah Loyd
Founding pastor, The Bridge Church, Portland, OR; adjunct professor at Warner Pacific College; and co-creator of Women's Convergence.

Made in the USA
San Bernardino, CA
19 April 2014